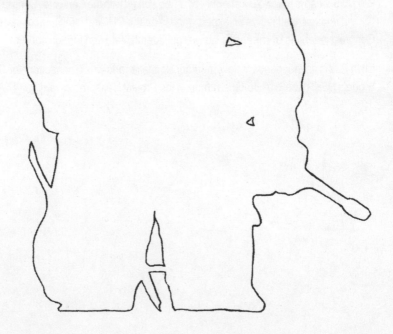

BIOTERROR

Manufacturing Wars The American Way

WILLIAM H. SCHAAP and ELLEN RAY were co-founders of *CovertAction Quarterly*, the authoritative magazine which has been a multiple award-winner of "Project Censored" prizes for its decades of groundbreaking investigative reporting.

William Schaap is a New York attorney, who has worked with the Center for Consitutional Rights, and has testified as an expert witness on the CIA and intelligence matters in Congressional and UN hearings, as well as federal, state and foreign courts.

Ellen Ray is an independent documentary filmmaker and was a consultant for Oliver Stone's "JFK." She is a two-time winner of the Project Censored Award.

BIOTERROR

Manufacturing Wars The American Way

Edited and with an Introduction by
Ellen Ray and William H. Schaap

**Published in association with the
Institute for Media Analysis, Inc.**

Ocean Press
Melbourne ■ New York
www.oceanbooks.com.au

ISBN 1-876175-64-8
Library of Congress Control Number: 2002115084
First Printed in Australia 2003

PUBLISHED BY OCEAN PRESS

Australia: GPO Box 3279, Melbourne, Victoria 3001, Australia
Fax: (61-3) 9329 5040   Tel: (61-3) 9326 4280
E-mail: info@oceanbooks.com.au

USA: PO Box 1186, Old Chelsea Station, New York, NY 10113-1186, USA
Tel: (718) 246-4160

OCEAN PRESS DISTRIBUTORS:

United States and Canada: *Consortium Book Sales and Distribution*
1045 Westgate Drive, Suite 90, Saint Paul, MN 55114-1065, USA
Tel: 1-800-283-3572

Britain and Europe: *Global Book Marketing*
38 King Street, London WC2E 8JT, UK

Australia and New Zealand: *Astam Books*
57-61 John Street, Leichhardt, NSW 2040, Australia

Cuba and Latin America: *Ocean Press*
Calle 21 #406, Vedado, Havana, Cuba

www.oceanbooks.com.au

CONTENTS

INTRODUCTION

Ellen Ray and William H. Schaap

"The Bush administration has provided the U.S. public with little more than rhetorically laced speculation... There has been nothing in the way of substantive fact presented that makes the case that Iraq possesses these weapons or has links to international terror, that Iraq poses a threat to the United States of America worthy of war."
— Scott Ritter, former UNSCOM weapons inspector in Iraq

"The absence of evidence is not the evidence of absence."
— Donald Rumsfeld, U.S. Secretary of Defense

As Washington prepared for a new war against Iraq and other nations declared to be part of the "Axis of Evil" for stockpiling weapons of mass destruction, the Bush administration abandoned an international effort to strengthen the Biological Weapons Convention against germ warfare. The *Washington Post* (September 19, 2002) warned, "the move will weaken attempts to curb germ warfare programs at a time when biological weapons are a focus of concern because of the war on terrorism and the administration's threats to launch a military campaign against Iraq."

The hypocrisy and dissembling of the U.S. Government is evident today not only in such actions and its language — "Weapons of Mass Destruction" (WMD) being the new, more militaristic buzzword — but also in the fact that the United States has been the only nation ever to have deployed the most lethal of WMDs, nuclear bombs, against civilians. Moreover, the United States has also been the most notorious and prolific practitioner of chemical-biological warfare (CBW) since World War II, endangering not just "target populations" but U.S. citizens and armed forces personnel as well.

The *Los Angeles Times* (October 10, 2002) reported that the United States itself had conducted up to 72 "tests," spraying VX, e.coli, sarin, tabun, soman and Agent Orange (among others) on civilians and military personnel in the United States, Canada and Europe in the 1960s and 1970s. In fact, much of Washington's prodigious capacity in this field stems from its secret acquisition of the gruesome CBW research data of its wartime foes, Germany and Japan, in return for which it suppressed its knowledge of these activities, not only in the war-crimes tribunals that followed the end of the war but for decades thereafter. It has also long been documented that the United States launched a CBW attack against the Chinese during the Korean War.

During the post-war decades, vast installations were developed at Fort Detrick in Maryland, at the Dugway Proving Grounds in Utah, and elsewhere, with special operations units of experimental scientists devoted to research, production, and testing of CBW agents and toxins. The official line has been that such work was "defensive" only, but there can be virtually no difference between offensive and defensive research in CBW.

Although such military research was highly classified, by 1975 concern over revelations of myriad intelligence abuses led to a comprehensive investigation by the U.S. Senate's Church Committee, which published a CIA memorandum listing the deadly chemical agents and toxins then stockpiled at Fort Detrick. These included anthrax, encephalitis, tuberculosis, lethal snake venom, shellfish toxin, and half a dozen lethal food poisons, some of which, the committee learned, had been shipped in the early 1960s to Congo and to Cuba in unsuccessful CIA attempts to assassinate Patrice Lumumba and Fidel Castro. And this was only what the U.S. Army was safekeeping for the CIA, not its own arsenal of CBW agents, known to include deadly and extremely dangerous binary nerve gas and other esoteric bio-killers.

In the wake of its unconscionable and devastating use of CBW during the Vietnam War, Washington repeatedly claimed that its enemies were either using or on the verge of using CBW. In the 1980s, the United States accused Vietnam of dropping so-called "yellow rain" in Cambodia; it accused the Soviet Union of using lethal chemicals in Afghanistan. It accused Iraq and Iran, at different times, of using nerve gas against each other. It similarly accused North Korea, Libya, Syria, and recently Al Qaeda of CBW/WMD capabilities. Many of these accusations were later shown to be outright intelligence disinformation hoaxes or to have involved substances the United States itself had supplied to one side or the other.

In the aftermath of the low-tech but deadly September 11 attacks, Washington launched a high-tech invasion of Afghanistan to destroy Al Qaeda and take its leader, Osama bin Laden, dead or alive. A year of indiscriminate carpet bombing — including of caves, remote villages, wedding parties, and a tribal delegation traveling to Kabul for the installation of a U.S.-sponsored provisional government — has left Afghanistan more dangerous and hopeless than before. Meanwhile, George W. Bush, Dick Cheney, and Donald Rumsfeld neither know nor seem to care whether bin Laden is alive or dead.

A remarkable policy shift occurred when Bush administration hardliners moved to phase two without explanation or apology for the dismal failure of phase one. The next focus of their apparently endless "new" war on terrorism was Iraq: the goal to remove Washington's former staunch ally, Saddam Hussein, from power in a pre-election campaign that demanded a higher level of military production (and profits) than the diminishing targets of Afghanistan. Control of Iraq, according to Cheney, would secure for the United States 10 percent of the world's oil production.

In launching this latest campaign Washington brushed aside in an instant the norms of international law, hundreds of years in the making. The Bush doctrines of "force resolution" and "anticipatory self-defense" — in other words, preemptive retaliation (the notion that the United States can attack an enemy simply because it might attack in the future) — are not new. His father invaded Panama, which posed no threat whatsoever to the United States, discarding yet another former collaborator, Manuel Noriega.

During the Reagan-Bush years, and earlier, Israel honed preemption to a fine edge, applying it in its internal struggle against the Palestinians and against virtually all its Arab neighbors, generally with U.S. acquiescence. Yet, when Israel bombed the Iraqi nuclear reactor at Osirak in 1981, a preemptive action it justified as "self-defense," the United States joined a UN resolution condemning the attack, even as it was supplying the industrial-scale chemical weapons that found their way to the battlefields of the Iran-Iraq War.

Although the United States is a signatory to the 1972 Biological Weapons Convention, the Bush administration refused to accept the 1997 protocol on verification of compliance. While Washington demanded that Iraq and any other country accused of CBW capacity open its doors to inspectors, it rejected the protocol because it would grant foreign inspectors too much access to U.S. installations and companies. It might expose, they argued, legitimate U.S. military and commercial secrets. And now, in its war fever, Washington takes the position that inspectors in Iraq would be ineffective.

In April 2002, the U.S. Government forced the resignation of the director of the Organization for the Prohibition of Chemical Weapons, alleging he was mismanaging the organization, but the real concern was his efforts to persuade Iraq to sign the convention and allow UN inspections, which could have removed one of the administration's main justifications for a "preemptive" attack against that country. Washington's true agenda, no longer secret in light of its frenzy of accusations against Iraq, is the imperial notion that U.S. "preparedness" includes the inalienable right of preemptive retaliation.

Rarely is it acknowledged that during the 1980s, when relations between the United States and Iraq were restored, it was Washington that supplied Iraq with more than a dozen biological and chemical agents with military potential, almost all of the material now suspected of use by Iraq in bioweapons research. At the same time the United States went so far as to veto a UN resolution condemning chemical warfare there. Donald Rumsfeld, now Secretary of Defense, was President Reagan's personal envoy who reestablished those relations and who oversaw the resumption of such chemical munitions trade, in an effort to prevent Iran's victory in the Iran-Iraq War. Rumsfeld was in Baghdad with Hussein the day that veto was cast. Under President George Bush (Snr.) U.S. support for Iraq intensified, as described in Jack Colhoun's article, only to terminate abruptly with Iraq's invasion of Kuwait and the commencement of the Gulf War.

Hawks in the current Bush administration recently floated the spurious accusation that the government of Cuba has "a limited capacity for germ warfare research," suggesting it could some day be used against the United States or provided to its enemies. Yet there has never been a hint of such research in Cuba, which is world-renowned for its bio-pharmaceutical laboratories. In the face of White House disapproval, former President Jimmy Carter visited Cuba in the spring of 2002 at the height of the accusations and toured some of these facilities. He announced there was no evidence of any CBW research, causing a Bush administration official to admit there were "difficulties" in proving the allegation.

Then, in mid-September, as war drums along the Potomac rose in intensity, Undersecretary of State John Bolton, a former Jesse Helms protégé, leaked to a right-wing scandal sheet the latest disinformation line from the White House, alleging that Cuban CBW might be responsible for the West Nile virus epidemic. Bolton based his claim on a document he said was to be given to the Senate Intelligence Committee, a document supposedly suppressed. The outbreaks of the virus had been traced to birds that "may have been infected at Cuban bioweapons labs," Bolton stated.

As part of this new wave of disinformation, Deputy Assistant Secretary of State Dan Fisk claimed that Cuba was intentionally disrupting U.S. efforts to combat terrorism. Both allegations have been vigorously denied by the Cuban Government, but the fact that such preposterous claims are being raised does not bode well for the peace and security of Cuba. Cuba, in fact, has for more than 40 years been the victim of deadly U.S. biological warfare, not the perpetrator, as is described in detail in the article on dengue fever in this book.

The specter of smallpox is also again haunting the world. More than 20 years after it was virtually wiped off the face of the globe, fear of a smallpox epidemic is in the headlines because neither the United

States nor the Soviet Union agreed to destroy the small amounts of the bacteria kept in laboratories after the elimination of the disease. The security of such samples, it now transpires, has been astonishingly lax, and no one knows who might have stolen some.

It is further irony that the only people ever in history to use smallpox as a weapon are the Americans whose colonial forebears, as early as the 1760s, gave blankets laced with smallpox to the indigenous inhabitants of the land they were rapidly expropriating. Thousands of Native Americans were killed by this virulent disease, to which they had never before been exposed. The tactic was repeated by the U.S. Army in the Indian Wars of the mid- and late-19th century, a history described in Ken Lawrence's overview.

As part of its new imperial strategy and war fever, the United States is now leading a hysterical campaign of "preparedness," ostensibly against terrorists — or whomever it labels as terrorists — who might use the scourge of smallpox or similar diseases as a bioweapon. The multibillion dollar Bioterrorism Preparedness Act, signed into law in June 2002, allocates more than $600 million to produce and stockpile vaccines for everyone in the United States. The Food and Drug Administration has suspended its basic requirement of advance human testing.

Originally, the plan called for offering the vaccine to every U.S. citizen, but shortly after the act was passed the Advisory Committee on Immunization Practices rejected the proposal and called for the immunization of only about 15,000 "first responders," those health care and law enforcement workers who would be likely involved in responding to a biological attack. Adverse reactions, to both smallpox and anthrax vaccinations, including serious illness and death, are statistically very high.

The act exempts from disclosure under the Freedom of Information Act the locations and users of bio-agents and toxins, making it more difficult for opponents of CBW research to object to specific projects, or to learn of accidents at or thefts from CBW installations. New government regulations, designed to limit access to certain materials to those scientists and students approved by the administration, are leading some universities to consider rejecting new government research work. Defense Department regulations are designed to control the publications, speech, and travel of scientists who accept Pentagon research funds.

The articles that follow appeared in *CovertAction* magazine between 1982 and 1993. The first two, Ken Lawrence's "History of U.S. Bio-Chemical Killers," and Bob Lederer's "Chemical-Biological Warfare, Medical Experiments, and Population Control," provide an overview of the history of U.S. chemical and biological warfare, noted above. This sordid history bears some study; it has been steady and consistent, usually secret, and not always directed against foreign nations. And its sweep has been grand, if perverse, as Richard Hatch's article, "Cancer Warfare," demonstrates.

Another article, extremely significant in light of recent developments, is Dr. Meryl Nass's analysis of "Zimbabwe's Anthrax Epizootic" of 1978. In the anthrax scare shortly after the September 11 attacks, five people died in the United States; this has yet to be explained. For nearly a year the FBI made virtually no headway. The administration originally tried to shield its apparent ineptitude from media scrutiny by accusing both Saddam Hussein and Al Qaeda of possessing the deadly microbe. Yet the U.S. Government alone possesses the precise strain of anthrax used in the letter mailings, with which it has been experimenting at Dugway for many years.

While most investigators concluded the attacks were homegrown, probably involving a U.S. scientist or bio-researcher, this U.S. terrorism has never been part of any international dialogue on CBW and WMD. The U.S. Government rejected a proposal that the UN Security Council condemn the attacks in order to eliminate any call for an international investigation.

During the spring and summer of 2002, however, the *New York Times* columnist Nicholas Kristof published a series of articles about "Mr. X," a former U.S. Army biological researcher, of whom the FBI had been aware since October, and who should have been a prime suspect. He noted that Mr. X (revealed by Kristof as Dr. Steven J. Hatfill) had worked with the infamous Selous Scouts of Ian Smith's racist regime in Rhodesia (where he got his medical degree) and with the South African Defense Force under its apartheid government. At that time he claimed he was working for the U.S. Special Forces in Africa, and that he was an innocent patriot.

There has been no public discussion of the events in Rhodesia during Hatfill's time there, but, as Dr. Nass's investigation notes, during the final years of the war of independence against the racist Smith regime, there was an unusually severe anthrax epidemic that killed vast numbers of black farmers. What role the patriotic Dr. Hatfill had in that disaster, or the current anthrax scare, remains to be seen, but it is difficult to imagine that either was the work of a sole culprit. Ironically, although Hatfill has been classified as a "person of interest" by Attorney General Ashcroft, his name appeared in the long-dormant list of UN registered weapons inspectors, from whom the team to go to Iraq was to be chosen.

The next three articles describe other examples of U.S. chemical-biological warfare. "The 1981 Cuba Dengue Epidemic," describes in detail the introduction of a widespread and deadly epidemic into Cuba by the CIA and its Cuban-exile agents. A. Namika's "Agent Orange: The Dirty Legal War at Home," and Tod Ensign's "Gulf War Syndrome: Guinea Pigs and Disposable GIs," both recount an equally tragic aspect of America's use of CBW in the process of waging secret and illegal chemical wars against foreign enemies, Vietnam in the case of Agent Orange, a deadly toxic defoliant, and Iraq in the case of depleted uranium, a radioactive component of powerful U.S. antitank missiles. In both wars, the "collateral damage" was to unwitting U.S. GIs who deployed these weapons. Hundreds and thousands of veterans returned home with the growing degenerative effects of working in close proximity to these chemicals building in their bodies. Because of the inherent secrecy, the U.S. Government was loath to admit any responsibility, or indeed any problem, and the U.S. victims have had to fight for years, often with little success, for recognition or recompense. Of course the millions of victims in Vietnam and in Iraq would be beyond the scope of reparations.

Finally, in "Bush Administration Uses CIA to Stonewall Iraqgate Investigations," Jack Colhoun details how the first Bush administration fought a member of Congress to prevent the disclosure of the weapons it supplied Iraq. Sales and loans were authorized up to the very day of the invasion of Kuwait, with many huge U.S. corporations profiting handsomely.

In light of those very dealings, the U.S. rush to war, calling for a "regime change" in Iraq, should be viewed as transparently imperialistic. In accusing Iraq of the capacity to produce WMD, vague allegations of Iraq's ability to produce nuclear weapons sometime in the future were raised, with no evidence of possession of or intention to use those weapons against the United States and none of any preparations to use chemical and biological agents against the United States, Israel, or any other country. Iraq had not, critics pointed out, employed CBW during the first Gulf War, as had been feared. Nevertheless, by its actions, the Bush administration is putting U.S. citizens, people in the Middle East, and indeed the whole world at risk.

As more and more information emerges, the articles in this book shed historical light on the audacity of Washington's accusations about the threat posed by WMDs today. We hope they help point the finger of blame where it belongs. Where it has belonged for 250 years, since Native Americans became the first victims of CBW.

New York
October 2002

THE HISTORY OF U.S. BIO-CHEMICAL KILLERS

Ken Lawrence

The involvement of the United States with chemical-biological warfare began in 1763 when blankets poisoned with smallpox were presented as gifts to Indians who sought only friendly relations with the colonists. It reached its peak 200 years later when the U.S. Air Force blanketed the countryside of Indochina with poisons whose effects are still being felt.

Chemical-biological warfare did not originate in North America, of course. It dates back to the poisoned arrows and smoke screens of antiquity. But its use by the United States has been persistent, and especially savage. The genocidal use of smallpox against Native Americans begun in colonial days was repeated during the later "Trail of Tears" era of the early and middle 19th century.

The World War I Experience

Chemical warfare came into its own during World War I. Incapaci-tating and poisonous gases were employed by all the belligerent powers almost from the war's outset. Nevertheless, it is significant that even though the United States entered the war only in its last year, and employed far fewer weapons than the other powers, a much higher percentage of U.S. artillery was devoted to chemical weapons than was true for the others. Of gas shells fired as a proportion of total artillery ammunition, the figure for the United States was 12 percent, while the next highest was Germany at 6.4 percent; the U.S. Army's Chemical Warfare Service (CWS) boasts, "By November 1918, the United States was manufacturing almost as much gas as England and France combined and nearly four times as much as Germany, which at the start of the war had led all other nations in the field of chemistry."

After the war ended, the United States was involved in two attempts to proscribe chemical weapons. General Pershing himself initiated a 1921 proposal that would have outlawed all use of poison gas, and it was actually ratified by the Senate, but fell through when France failed to ratify. Four years later, however, the Senate refused to ratify the Geneva Gas Protocol, and in 1926 Secretary of State Frank B. Kellogg declared U.S. policy "to be fully prepared as regards chemical war-fare," even though most other countries did ratify the protocol. Meanwhile, beginning in 1922 with an appropriation of $1,350,000, Congress gave an annual amount to the CWS which gradually grew as World War II approached.

For a time the CWS was barred from procuring and stockpiling weapons (though not from research, development, and procurement planning), but in 1935 and 1936, following reports that Italy had employed poison gas during its conquest of Ethiopia, Congress explicitly designated its appropriation for "manufacture of chemical warfare gases or other toxic substances — or other offensive or defensive materials required for gas warfare purposes."

World War II Stockpiles

Although poison gas was not used in battle during World War II, except by the Japanese against China (and possibly a few times against

U.S. troops in New Guinea), both the Axis and the Allies had stockpiled large arsenals of chemical weapons, and the Germans had developed and secretly begun to manufacture two kinds of nerve gas, tabun and sarin. Both sides seriously considered employing gas and bacteriological warfare. Adolf Hitler's plans were thwarted by his commanders who feared retaliation in kind. Winston Churchill's secret order of July 6, 1944, revealed just recently, read: "It may be several weeks, or even months, before I shall ask you to drench Germany with poison gas, and if we do it, let us do it 100 percent. In the meanwhile, I want the matter studied in cold blood by sensible people and not by that particular set of psalm-singing uniformed defeatists which one runs across now here now there." By this time his general staff advised against the use of gas. Earlier Britain's Chiefs of Staff had planned to use gas against the expected German invasion that never happened, and the United States, while still officially neutral in mid-1941, secretly manufactured phosgene gas and shipped it to Britain.

Official U.S. policy was to use gas only in retaliation. On June 8, 1943, President Roosevelt told the press that, "We shall under no circumstances resort to the use of such weapons unless they are first used by our enemies." But secretly the option of first use remained available. Admiral Chester Nimitz and the combined Chiefs of Staff approved poison gas during the invasion of Iwo Jima, but were overruled by the president. There was also a contingency plan to use gas had the United States gone ahead with the plan to invade Japan, scrapped at the last minute in favor of the atom bomb. Despite the president's statement, the planners at the War Department lived with "the conviction that gas warfare was all but inevitable," according to the CWS official history.

Summing up in the recent book, *A Higher Form of Killing*, Robert Harris and Jeremy Paxman wrote, "The world missed chemical warfare in the Second World War by inches." Apparently, it missed large-scale biological warfare by an even smaller margin, and in a number of instances there is strong evidence that this form of warfare probably was employed: by Japanese against people, crops, and livestock in China; by the United States against crops in Germany and Japan; by the British in the assassination of Nazi leader Reinhard

Heydrich; and in the use of infectious diseases and poison by anti-Nazi partisans in Eastern Europe.

Germ Warfare and Nuremberg

The United States and Britain, in 1944 or earlier, planned to attack six major German cities — Berlin, Hamburg, Stuttgart, Frankfurt, Wilhelmshafen, and Aachen — with anthrax bombs that would have killed half their populations. The bombs were ordered to be produced at a factory in Vigo, Indiana, but the hazards of production delayed start-up, and the war was over before the bombs could be manufactured. The British had, however, stockpiled five million cattle cakes poisoned with anthrax for use against the enemy's livestock by the war's end. The United States went on to develop delivery systems to spread brucellosis, a highly infectious organism which is rarely fatal but incapacitates its victims with "chills and undulating fever, headache, loss of appetite, mental depression, extreme exhaustion, aching joints, and sweating," sometimes for up to a year. Virtually everyone associated with the program fell sick for a time.

Unlike chemical warfare, which had been banned by the 1925 Geneva Gas Protocol that Britain had ratified and the United States had not, neither country considered biological warfare to be illegal, and at least one secret U.S. memo quoted by Harris and Paxman called it "very humane indeed." This later posed a problem for the Western allies: At the end of the war, the Soviet Union pressed for the death penalty for one of the Nuremberg defendants, Hans Fritzsche, on the grounds that he had first suggested the possibility of germ warfare to the German High Command. For Britain and America it was an acutely embarrassing moment. By 1945 they were aware that they had invested vastly more time and effort in producing these "forbidden weapons" than the Nazis. They insisted — to the fury of the Russians — that Fritzsche be acquitted.

After World War II

The next reasonably well-documented instance of germ warfare occurred during the Korean War. In February 1952, the Democratic People's Republic of Korea and the People's Republic of China charged that U.S. pilots had dropped "germ bombs" on North Korea. They offered as evidence the testimony of captured U.S. Air Force officers and intelligence agents, and Koreans who told of finding large quantities of fleas and other insect pests shortly after U.S. planes had flown over their areas. The U.S. Government strenuously denied the charge, but a respected group of scientists believed the evidence was convincing proof that the United States had employed biological weapons.

"The International Scientific Commission for the Investigation of the Facts Concerning Bacteriological Warfare in Korea and China" included scientists from Great Britain, France, Italy, Sweden, Brazil, and the Soviet Union. One of the most renowned scientists of the 20th century, Joseph Needham of England, sat on the commission. Its 700-page report described a whole array of germ weapons: feathers infected with anthrax; lice, fleas, and mosquitoes dosed with plague and yellow fever; diseased rodents; and various implements contaminated with deadly microbes — toilet paper, envelopes, and the ink in fountain pens.

In 1958 the Eisenhower administration pressed sedition charges against three Americans who had published the germ warfare charge in *China Monthly Review* — John W. Powell, Sylvia Powell, and Julian Schuman — but failed to get convictions.

The Vietnam War

When the bicentennial of U.S. chemical-biological warfare came in the early 1960s, the U.S. Government marked the occasion with the most massive chemical war waged by any power in world history. Even today the people of Indochina are suffering the long-term effects of those chemicals on their land, crops, livestock, and persons. Ironically, a large number of U.S. military personnel involved in the Indochina war have also suffered serious harm from those same chemicals, especially Agent Orange.

The use of chemical defoliants was approved by President Kennedy on November 30, 1961, following a recommendation by Secretary of State Dean Rusk that the way to win a war against a guerrilla army is to destroy crops. General William C. Westmoreland also considered crop destruction an important aspect of U.S. strategy, pointing out in a secret report that spraying 13,800 acres would destroy "crops which if allowed to grow until harvest might feed 15,000 soldiers for a year."

By the end of the war, 55 million kilograms of chemical defoliants had been dropped on Indochina, mainly Agent Orange (a mixture of two herbicides plus small but toxic amounts of dioxin, a substance considered 100 times as poisonous as cyanide), also including Agent White, especially persistent in soil, and Agent Blue, which contains arsenic and is thought to be responsible for the poisoning of many Vietnamese peasants.

Nine million kilograms of anti-personnel gases were also employed, mainly CS gas, which was used to flush enemy soldiers and civilians out of their shelters so they could be captured and shot. In closed quarters, such as caves, these so-called "riot control" chemicals can kill or maim directly, as was commonplace in Vietnam. Besides CS, there is strong evidence that, on at least three occasions, U.S. forces also used BZ gas, a hallucinogen that causes breathing difficulty, blurred vision, dizziness, disorientation, loss of memory, and erratic, aggressive behavior.

The use of chemical weapons in Indochina was more open than the germ warfare waged against North Korea, but it was still deceptive. In 1971, Major General Bernard Rogers wrote to Senator J. William Fulbright that defoliation operations in Vietnam "are of limited scope and are subject to the same regulations applied to herbicide use in the United States." General Rogers, now NATO commander, must have known this was a lie. Five million acres, 12 percent of South Vietnam, were sprayed at an application rate that averaged 13 times the amounts recommended by the U.S. Department of Agriculture.

Few details of this war would have become public, but for its immense scale. Secretary of Defense Robert McNamara wanted the spraying disguised as a program conducted by South Vietnamese civilians, and his Deputy Undersecretary U. Alexis Johnson proposed that "U.S. aircraft be used to conduct a major defoliant spray program in South Vietnam, although the aircraft would carry South Vietnamese markings and the pilots would wear civilian clothes." The actual scope of the chemical attack against Laos, opposed even by then U.S. Ambassador William H. Sullivan, was kept secret until this past January [1982], and some of the details are still classified. In fact, the Joint Chiefs of Staff noted in a 1961 document that "care must be taken to assure that the United States does not become the target for charges of employing chemical or biological warfare. International repercussions could be most serious."

Although the main victims of these weapons are the people of Indochina, thousands who suffer the results of dioxin poisoning — weakness of the eyes and some actual blindness, muscle weakness, liver damage, cancer, and a high rate of miscarriage and infant malformation, including hundreds of babies born without eyes — the harmful effects would probably have vanished from the pages of the [U.S.] press were it not for the vast number of former GIs, 60,000 of them, who are suffering the same symptoms. But even their plight, which ought to serve as a monument to the horrors of chemical-biological warfare, is not deterring our government from embarking on its third century of germ and chemical warfare with all the attendant lies and deceit.

1982

CHEMICAL-BIOLOGICAL WARFARE, MEDICAL EXPERIMENTS, AND POPULATION CONTROL

Robert Lederer

U.S. history is replete with efforts to inflict disease and death on Third World peoples, both inside and outside U.S. borders, through chemical-biological warfare, medical experiments, and population control. And despite an alleged "ban" on development of chemical-biological warfare weapons since 1969, there is also ample evidence that such programs have continued, incorporating the latest techniques in genetic engineering. In addition, the U.S. military has never shown any compunction about testing chemical-biological warfare techniques on the general population in this country.

Chemical-Biological Warfare: Some History

Chemical warfare is the use of chemicals to kill, incapacitate, or harm humans, animals or plants; biological warfare is the use of disease-causing germs to do the same thing. Chemical-biological warfare is simply a further extension of other military, economic, and political measures directed against the peoples of "enemy" nations.

U.S. chemical-biological warfare has been used primarily for counterinsurgency operations against Third World peoples struggling for self-determination, and destabilization of Third World governments which have thwarted U.S. domination. During the world wars, chemical-biological warfare was also directed against U.S. adversaries.

More recent incidents in which the involvement of U.S. chemical-biological warfare is so far unconfirmed include the following:

El Salvador: In 1982, Salvadoran trade unionists charged that epidemics of previously unknown diseases had erupted in many areas immediately after U.S.-directed aerial bombings. Particularly cited was hemorrhagic conjunctivitis, which causes bleeding of the eyes.[1] In 1985, the Salvadoran Association of Health Professionals charged that another new disease, which caused high fevers, headaches, joint pains, rash, and later jaundice, occurred after bombings "of an unfamiliar character." In both cases, U.S. chemical-biological warfare was suspected.[2]

Nicaragua: In 1985, an outbreak of dengue fever — the first such epidemic in the country — occurred in Managua and other areas a few months after the escalation of U.S. aerial reconnaissance missions. Nearly half of the capital city's population became ill, and there were several deaths. The Nicaraguan Health Ministry has been investigating the possibility of a U.S. chemical-biological warfare role.[3]

It should also be mentioned that some black and Latino activists in the United States have called drug smuggling and distribution in Third World communities a form of chemical warfare. As they note, it is no accident that heroin in particular began flooding those communities at the height of the urban rebellions of the late 1960s. The CIA involvement in the Southeast Asian heroin trade and, more recently, Latin American cocaine smuggling, has been well documented.

Less well known is the major role of U.S. urban police forces in allowing and sometimes participating in drug sales.[4]

Chemical-Biological Warfare Tests in the United States

Tests of chemical-biological warfare agents, often performed without the knowledge of human subjects, have been carried out for decades on both individuals and entire populations.[5] Many of these programs were exposed in the mid- and late-1970s through media and congressional investigations and Freedom of Information Act lawsuits. The most famous program was MKULTRA, one of several CIA and army projects seeking to perfect mind control and incapacitating agents. Many of the drugs tested had been rejected by pharmaceutical companies due to their undesirable side effects. In the 1950s and 1960s, scores of such drugs, including LSD, were tested on military personnel and prisoners.

Other common chemical-biological warfare tests included open-air experiments spraying what were claimed to be harmless agents. In 1977, the army admitted carrying out hundreds of such tests since World War II, including 25 targeting the public. On 48 occasions between 1951 and 1967, the army employed microbes known to be disease-causing agents in open-air tests, and it used disease-causing anti-crop substances 31 times. Some especially outrageous highlights:

- In 1950, the U.S. Navy sprayed a cloud of bacteria over San Francisco. The navy claimed the bacteria used in the simulated attack were harmless, but many residents came down with pneumonia-like symptoms and one died.
- In 1952 and 1953, clouds of zinc cadmium sulfide were sprayed over Winnipeg, Manitoba; St. Louis, Missouri; Minneapolis, Minnesota; Fort Wayne, Indiana; the Monocacy River Valley in Maryland; and Leesburg, Virginia. Despite claims of harmlessness, a military report noted respiratory problems.
- In 1955, the Tampa Bay area of Florida experienced a sharp rise in whooping cough cases, including 12 deaths, following a CIA biowar test whose details are still secret, involving bacteria withdrawn from an army chemical-biological warfare center.

- From 1956 to 1958, in the poor black communities of Savannah, Georgia, and Avon Park, Florida, the army carried out field tests with mosquitoes that may have been infected with yellow fever. The insects were released into residential areas from ground level and dropped from planes and helicopters. Many people were swarmed by mosquitoes and then developed unknown fevers; some died. After each test, army agents posing as public health officials photographed and tested victims and then disappeared from town.[6]

- From June 7 to 10, 1966, the U.S. Army's Special Operations Division dispensed a bacillus throughout the New York City subway system. The army's report on the experiment noted the existence of subways in the Soviet Union, Europe, and South America.

- In 1968 and 1969, the CIA experimented with the possibility of poisoning drinking water systems by injecting a chemical substance into the water supply of the Food and Drug Administration building in Washington.

- In 1976, the Humane Society of Utah questioned the mysterious deaths of 50 wild horses that had drunk from a spring near the U.S. Army's Dugway Proving Ground, a chemical-biological warfare research center.

Deadly "Civilian" Medical Experiments

Besides the tests directly related to chemical-biological warfare, there has been a notorious history of deadly "civilian" medical experiments, often practiced on Third World peoples, and usually without their consent. Numerous new drugs have been tested on people in Third World nations long before such tests would be permitted in this country. For example, the birth control pill was first used on Puerto Rican and Haitian women in trials by the G.D. Searle pharmaceutical company in 1956.[7] The women were neither told what they were taking nor warned about the possible side effects, which the company knew to be potentially severe.

Within the United States and its direct colonies, there is a long history of experiments on prisoners using drugs — especially psychotropic ones — and toxic chemicals.[8] For example, early in this century, a North American doctor infected several prisoners with plague in the then-U.S. colony of the Philippines. He also produced beriberi in another group of 29 prisoners, two of whom died as a result of the experiments. In 1915, a doctor produced pellagra in 12 white Mississippi inmates in an attempt to discover a cure for the disease. In the 1940s, over 400 Chicago prisoners were infected with malaria as part of a wartime crash program to develop new drugs against this infection. In 1947, Nazi doctors on trial at Nuremberg for crimes against humanity cited some of these cases as precedents for their own genocidal experiments.[9] From 1965 to 1968, 70 prisoners, mostly black, at Holmesburg State Prison in Philadelphia, were the subjects of tests by Dow Chemical Company of the effects of dioxin, the highly toxic chemical contaminant in Agent Orange. Their skins were deliberately exposed to large doses and then monitored to watch the results. According to the doctor in charge, Albert Kligman, a University of Pennsylvania dermatologist, several subjects developed lesions which "lasted for four to seven months, since no effort was made to speed healing by active treatment." At a 1980 federal Environmental Protection Agency hearing where the experiment came to light, Kligman testified that no follow-up was done on subjects for possible development of cancer. This was the second such experiment commissioned by Dow, the previous one carried out on 51 "volunteers," believed also to have been prisoners.[10] A series of experiments that bears particular scrutiny were the mind-altering drug tests and aversion therapy measures, including electroshock treatment, used on prisoners in the California prisons of Vacaville and Atascadero in the 1960s.[11] Two of the most notorious and genocidal experiments in U.S. history are especially worth recalling:

Tuskegee Syphilis Study: In 1932, the U.S. Public Health Service initiated a study of untreated tertiary (third stage) syphilis using poor, uneducated black men in Tuskegee, Alabama. Four hundred syphilitics were never told of their illness and were denied treatment. Another 200 healthy black men were used as control subjects. Both groups were carefully monitored. According to the authoritative book on the subject, *Bad Blood*, by James H. Jones, "as of 1969, at least 28 and perhaps as many as 100 men had died as a direct result of complications caused by syphilis. Others had developed syphilis-related heart conditions that may have contributed to their deaths."[12] Many wives of the untreated men may also have been infected; some children may have been born with congenital defects.

The experiment continued until 1972, when an outraged federal worker blew the whistle to the press, and nationwide condemnation forced the government to cancel the project. This employee had protested privately as far back as 1966, only provoking increasingly high-level secret meetings which resolved to continue the project. In 1972, as they reluctantly ordered its end, federal health officials hypocritically joined the press denunciations while implicitly defending the study as legitimate in its time. The survivors still received no treatment until eight months later, on the eve of congressional hearings. The federal office supervising the study was the predecessor of one of today's Centers for Disease Control units. The CDC, a journalist wrote in 1972, "sees the poor, the black, the illiterate and the defenseless in American society as a vast experimental resource for the government."[13]

Puerto Rican Cancer Experiment: In 1931, Cornelius Rhoads, a North American pathologist at the Rockefeller Institute for Medical Investigations in San Juan, carried out a murderous "experiment" in which 13 Puerto Ricans died after being purposely infected with cancer. In a letter to another doctor, leaked to the Puerto Rican Nationalist Party, Rhoads wrote:

> the Porto Ricans [sic]... are beyond doubt the dirtiest, laziest, most degenerate and thievish race of men ever inhabiting this sphere. It makes you sick to inhabit the same island with them... What the island needs is not public health work, but a tidal wave or something to totally exterminate the population. It might then be livable. I have done my best to further the process of extermination by killing off eight and transplanting cancer into several more. The latter has not resulted in any fatalities so far... The matter of consideration for the patients' welfare plays no role here — in fact, all physicians take delight in the abuse and torture of the unfortunate subjects.[14]

The Nationalist Party President, Don Pedro Albizu Campos, brought the case to the press, the Puerto Rican Medical Association, and the League of Nations, but no action was taken. The North American

Governor of Puerto Rico had a prosecutor investigate the charge. Rhoads never denied writing the letter. And despite evidence proving that indeed 13 patients had died, eight of whom were treated by Rhoads, the prosecutor exonerated Rhoads, calling him merely "a mentally ill person or a man with few scruples."

But the story did not end there. This "mentally ill person" went on to direct the establishment of army chemical warfare laboratories in Maryland, Utah, and the Panama Canal Zone, for which he was awarded the Legion of Merit in 1945. That same year, Rhoads was appointed to the staff of the U.S. Atomic Energy Commission. The commission was at that time carrying out radiation experiments on unwitting prisoners, hospital patients, and soldiers. Meanwhile, between 1937 and 1947, Albizu and other nationalist leaders had been imprisoned for sedition after the pro-independence upsurge of the late 1930s. A 1950 island-wide nationalist insurrection led to the rearrest of Albizu and hundreds of activists. This time, he charged, several parts of his body were repeatedly subjected to radiation, burning, and he was being poisoned. Other nationalist prisoners later charged they were experimented on with drugs. According to Nationalist Party leaders, Rhoads was finally getting his revenge for Albizu's earlier murder charge.

Albizu was denounced by United States and local colonial officials as a lunatic, but doctors eventually supported his charges. His health steadily deteriorated, and he died shortly after his release from prison in 1965. Subsequent documents have been obtained supporting both his original murder charges and his allegations of radiation poisoning.

The New Age of Chemical-Biological Warfare

In 1969, under mounting pressure from the international and domestic antiwar movements, President Nixon announced a ban on the production and use of biological (but not chemical) warfare agents. In 1972, the United States signed an international treaty with similar provisions. It was not until Senate ratification in 1975 that the treaty took legal force in the United States. The Pentagon claims that these new policies meant the end of all but "defensive" biological warfare research. But this distinction is meaningless, as numerous chemical-biological warfare experts (including some of the army's own, before the ban) have attested.[15] This is because the studies required to protect against chemical-biological warfare are indistinguishable from those necessary to prepare microorganisms for attack. The fact that offensive programs continued is also shown by the documented biological attacks on Cuba in 1971 and 1981. It is also suggested by the incidents in Nicaragua and El Salvador described above.

Genetic Engineering: Newest Chemical-Biological Warfare Tool

In 1973, the new field of genetic engineering — combining molecules of different microorganisms to create new viruses and bacteria — was opened by advances in scientific research. The U.S. military applied this new technology to its chemical-biological warfare research. Many scientists warned of the extremely dangerous implications of such a development. While the military claims to be using genetic engineering only to develop vaccines (as is being done in the pharmaceutical industry), there is every reason to believe it is also being developed for offensive purposes.[16]

In February 1987, a lawsuit by the Foundation for Economic Trends, a Washington, D.C., environmental group, forced the Department of Defense (DoD) to admit the operation of chemical-biological warfare research programs (all "defensive" of course) at 127 sites around the country, including universities, foundations and corporations. *Science* magazine reported that the suit revealed that "DoD is applying recombinant DNA techniques in research and the production of a range of pathogens and toxins including botulism, anthrax, and yellow fever."[17] According to the foundation, this research effort increased dramatically in the past five years, but DoD had not examined the health effects of these activities as required by law. In the out-of-court settlement of that suit, the Pentagon agreed to file environmental impact statements on all of those programs within 21 months, to indicate any possible health risks to surrounding communities.

The Search for the Ultimate Bioweapon

The military has several times expressed its fantasies for new biological weapons. In 1969, a military official testified before Congress:

Within the next five or 10 years, it would probably be possible to make a new infective microorganism which could differ in certain important respects from any known disease-causing organisms. Most important of these is that it might be refractory [resistant] to the immunological and therapeutic processes upon which we depend to maintain our relative freedom from infectious disease.[18]

In a book on chemical-biological warfare, two authors commented on this testimony:

The possibility that such a "super germ" may have been successfully produced in a laboratory somewhere in the world in the years since that assessment was made is one which should not be too readily cast aside... This is not an entirely academic speculation. In 1968 Porton Down [the British Army's Biological Warfare Laboratory] and Fort Detrick collaborated in the successful transfer of genes between different strains of plague bacillus. The research was done "for purely defensive purposes."[19]

A 1985 U.S. Government study showed an awareness of the potential of genetic engineering. "The rapid advances of genetic technology — in which the United States for now is fortunately [sic] the leader — offer the predictable likelihood of new agents being developed for which no vaccines or counteragents are known or available."[20]

Another twist on chemical-biological warfare development is the prospect, predicted in a 1975 military manual, of "ethnic chemical weapons which would be designed to exploit naturally occurring differences in vulnerability among specific population groups."[21]

Population Control

Population control of the Third World has been a policy goal of U.S. officials for many years. In 1977, Ray Ravenhott, director of the population program of the U.S. Agency for International Development (AID), publicly announced his agency's goal was to sterilize one quarter of the world's women. He admitted, in essence, that this was necessary to protect U.S. corporate interests from the threat of revolutions spawned by chronic unemployment.[22]

Long before Ravenhott's statement, AID programs had brought birth control and sterilization clinics to U.S. client states throughout the Third World, often in regions with no other health facilities. The most "successful" implementation of this program has been in the U.S. colony of Puerto Rico. Under U.S. occupation since 1898, this Latin American island nation has had very high unemployment, corporate-generated environmental pollution, and a strong independence movement. A U.S.-financed network of sterilization clinics has been growing for 50 years. Through intense anti-childbearing propaganda and outright deception, Puerto Rico today has the highest sterilization rate in the world: 39 percent of women of child-bearing age, 25 percent of men.[23]

1987

CANCER WARFARE

Richard Hatch

"Those who would increase the potency of biological weapons must search for improved methods of mass production of organisms, factors which will enhance the virulence, ways to prolong the storage life of living agents, ways to improve aerosol stability, and methods of producing variant organisms by recombination or by other means."
— Col. William D. Tigertt, former commander of the army's medical unit at Fort Detrick[1]

National Cancer Institute and the Fort Detrick Link

In 1969, President Richard Nixon ordered a halt to offensive biological warfare research and weapons stockpiling by the United States. The U.S. Army destroyed its toxins, viruses, and bacteria with heat and disinfectants by May 1972; the disposal of the scientific personnel was not so simple. Some of these biowarriors went to the CIA.[2] Others quickly found new support from the National Cancer Institute (NCI), particularly in its Virus Cancer Program (VCP).[3] The NCI funded and supervised some of the same scientists, universities, and contracting corporations — ostensibly for cancer research — which had conducted biological warfare research. Some of these medical research contracts ran simultaneously with the U.S. biological warfare program. When the military work ended, the civilian program continued to expand on the same critical areas outlined by Colonel Tigertt.

The NCI's Viral Cancer Program — a highly politicized public relations effort — was launched in 1971 with great fanfare as part of Nixon's War on Cancer. The stated aim of the program was to organize experiments aimed at finding cancer-causing viruses.

Apparently this agenda was compatible with the incorporation into various units of the VCP of possibly dozens of former U.S. biological warfare researchers who continued to study topics with potential military application. Potential cancer-causing viruses were collected, grown in huge amounts, and distributed through the VCP; thousands of animals were infected experimentally, and the aerosol distribution of carcinogenic viruses was studied.

Two former biological weapons facilities would play a large part in VCP. The U.S. Army's Fort Detrick in Frederick, Maryland, had been the "parent research and pilot plant center for biological warfare."[4] During the early 1960s, the CIA paid the facility $100,000 a year for biological weapons and chemical agents and their delivery systems. In Oakland, California, the Naval Biosciences Laboratory was involved in early experiments with plague and collaborated in massive open-air tests of biological warfare "simulants" in the San Francisco Bay Area in the 1950s. Former biological warfare specialists from both of these centers were deeply involved in all aspects of the VCP.

The University-Military Complex

Reflecting a common pattern of cooperation, much of the military-related research took place at institutions connected with or directly part of U.S. universities. The University of California is well known for its role in managing the two main U.S. nuclear weapons laboratories, the Los Alamos and Lawrence Livermore National Laboratories. Less well known is the fact that UC Berkeley also helps manage the Naval Biosciences Laboratory (NBL) — earlier called the

Naval Biological Laboratory. This connection became central to the VCP and continued after the ban on offensive biological weapons work.

Well before President Nixon ordered the conversion of the U.S. Army biological warfare center at Fort Detrick to civilian uses in 1971, this military facility was cooperating closely with UC.

From 1953 to 1968, the University of California, while managing the NBL, now at the Naval Supply Center, also had biological weapons contracts with the U.S. Army.[5] After U.S. treaty obligations would have prevented open research on mass production of dangerous viruses without a medical "cover," the VCP provided an ideal excuse to study "scale-up" problems.[6]

One of the first new priorities of the Fort Detrick facility after the ban was "the large-scale production of oncogenic [cancer-causing] and suspected oncogenic viruses."[7] Within a year, the NCI began mass production and within one 15-month period ending in June 1977, the VCP produced 60,000 liters of cancer-causing and immuno-suppressive viruses. Throughout the 1970s, U.S. "defensive" biological warfare efforts were increasingly aimed at the research and development of viral disease agents.[8]

The "seed stocks" for this massive production of viruses came from the Cell Culture Laboratory (CCL); the CCL was "physically located at the Naval Biosciences Laboratory" in Oakland, California.[9] Because this laboratory was financed in part by the NCI and linked to UC, it would become, in effect, a clearinghouse and central repository for vast quantities of potentially cancer-causing viruses and the tissues that might contain them. Thus, after the ban, the Naval Biosciences Lab at UC continued experimentation on biological agents, but under the guise of "defensive" research.

The VCP contract ran concurrently with the NBL's work on bubonic plague, Rift Valley fever, and meningitis. The NBL did other research for the U.S. Army's Fort Detrick, before the 1972 ban on offensive work.[10] The NBL also performed "much of the original research into plague during World War II." At least some NBL work was "listed only in restricted Pentagon research bulletins."[11]

The NBL/Cell Culture Laboratory project was supervised for the VCP by Drs. James Duff and Jack Gruber.[12] Duff had been a microbiologist at Fort Detrick for 12 years before joining the NCI. His biography lists research into clostridium botulinum toxins and psittacosis vaccines.[13] Botulinum toxins cause botulism food poisoning and are among the most toxic substances known. It was during Duff's tenure at Fort Detrick that the U.S. Army stockpiled botulinum toxin weapons.[14] There, too, the intensive study of psittacosis, or "parrot fever," resulted in the accidental infection of at least 12 workers while Duff was working there.[15] After serving for eight years at Fort Detrick, Gruber moved to the NCI. His biography lists work on "arthropod-borne viruses."[16] The United States stockpiled biological weapons based on one arthropod-borne virus and studied many others. He soon became Chair of the Program Resources and Logistics Advisory Group of the VCP, where he helped coordinate projects involving production of viruses, provision of test animals and the "biohazard safety program."[17] In 1984, Gruber became head of the Cancer Etiology Division of the National Institutes of Health (NIH).

It's in the Air

The field of "aerobiology," or the transmission of disease organisms through the air, is essentially an outgrowth of biological weapons research. The military objective of exposing many people to a biological warfare agent and the ready susceptibility to infection by inhaling these agents make aerosol weapons the most practical form of transmission. The NCI also studied aerosol transmission of viruses intensively. One such study, FS-57 "Aerosol Properties of Oncogenic Viruses," was funded at more than $100,000 a year. After the ban on offensive biological warfare research, the NCI and the Office of Naval Research jointly sponsored NBL experiments on the "Aerosol Properties of Potentially Oncogenic Viruses."[18] The NCI justified its aerosol research because its scientists often handled suspect cancer viruses in a highly concentrated form. A lab accident could release a mist of virus; NCI needed to understand and anticipate the danger. How the navy justified its interest is unknown, but if a new cancer-causing biological warfare agent was discovered, it would likely be delivered as an aerosol.

The line between aerosol and biological warfare research was often fine. The NCI project officer and former U.S. Air Force virologist, Dr.

Alfred Hellman, worked with Mark Chatigny, a research engineer at NBL and member of the NCI biohazards work group from the NBL.[19] Hellman also oversaw the 1971 $100,000 NBL study on the "physical and biological characteristics of viral aerosols." In 1961, the NBL had done similar research for Fort Detrick on the "stability and virulence of biological warfare aerosols."[20] Chatigny's NBL research into aerosol distribution of viruses would continue into the 1980s. Such overlapping of purposes raises serious questions about the wisdom of placing control of VCP viruses under the NBL.

More Aerosol Studies

While UC Berkeley appears to have been at the heart of aerosol biological weapons research, it was by no means alone. Other universities collaborated with the biological warfare effort while working on the VCP in parallel. From 1955 to 1965, the Ohio State University College of Medicine conducted research for Fort Detrick into the aerosol transmission of biological warfare agents including tularemia and Q fever.[21] In some of these studies, prisoners from the Ohio State Penitentiary were used as guinea pigs. Between 1952 and 1969, the affiliated Ohio State University Research Foundation had eight contracts with the U.S. Army for biological warfare research. Tularemia ("rabbit fever") and Q fever were ultimately stockpiled by the U.S. Army.[22]

Before he worked with UC, Dr. Hellman supervised an NCI contract for Ohio State University. Designed to study the aerosol transmission of cancer-causing viruses, this research started in 1965 and continued at least until 1972. The principal investigator for this work, Dr. Richard Griesemer, would eventually succeed in giving tumors to mice and monkeys. Griesemer then went to work briefly at the Oak Ridge National Laboratory, part of the U.S. Department of Energy nuclear research system. After his stint at Oak Ridge, Griesemer returned to NCI, where he headed the NCI Bioassay program, which tested chemicals suspected of causing cancer. This multimillion dollar program was so badly managed that disease epidemics forced the killing of nearly 90,000 test animals and testing of suspected carcinogenic chemicals fell far behind schedule.[23]

Many other universities prominent in the U.S. biological warfare program, such as Johns Hopkins, University of Maryland, and the University of Minnesota, were also heavily involved in the VCP. Since the biological warfare work performed by these universities remains classified, the exact relation between VCP and its biological warfare research remains murky.

Viruses For Sale — Charles Pfizer and Co., Inc.

The pattern of overlapping military biological weapons and NCI work was paralleled by the relationship between industrial contractors and the VCP. Charles Pfizer and Company, Inc., a pharmaceutical firm, had a contract with the NCI which included production of "a large quantity of a variety of viruses" for the VCP.[24] The immunosuppressive Mason-Pfizer monkey virus was grown in large quantities, and other animal cancer viruses were adapted to grow in human cell lines. During the same time period — 1961 to 1971 — as the NCI contractor, Pfizer conducted a secret study for the U.S. Army "into the growth and culture media for unspecified... biological agents."[25]

In addition, from 1968 to 1970, Pfizer had a contract for "Large Scale Production and Evaluation of Staphylococcal Enterotoxoid B" for the U.S. Army biological warfare program.[26] Staphylococcal Enterotoxoid is a protective vaccine against a bacterial toxin which was part of the U.S. arsenal. The production of vaccines against a stockpiled biological weapon must be considered an offensive biological warfare project. According to MIT scientists Harlee Strauss and Jonathan King, "[t]hese steps — the generation of a potential biological warfare agent, development of a vaccine against it, testing of the efficacy of the vaccine — are all components that would be associated with an offensive biological warfare program."[27] Clearly, without an antidote or vaccine to protect attacking troops, the utility of a stockpiled biological warfare agent would be seriously limited.

Litton-Bionetics

President Nixon's 1971 announcement that Fort Detrick would be converted to a center for cancer research could not be immediately implemented. First, biological warfare agents stored there, such as the anti-crop agent rice blast, had to be destroyed. The buildings were then decontaminated and the facilities were turned over to the NCI, which renamed the facility the Frederick Cancer Research Center; Litton-Bionetics was named as the prime contractor. A major player in the military-industrial complex, the corporation worked extensively on the dispersion of biological warfare agents from planes, and included U.S. Air Force contracts for "the supersonic delivery of dry biological agents."[28] From 1966 to 1968, Bionetics Research Laboratories (which became Litton-Bionetics in 1973) held two contracts with the U.S. Army biological warfare program.[29] At the same time, it held major contracts with the NCI.[30]

One of Bionetics Research Laboratories' most important NCI contracts was a massive virus inoculation program that began in 1962 and ran until at least 1976, and used more than 2,000 monkeys. Dr. Robert Gallo, the controversial head of the current U.S. AIDS research program at NCI and chief of its tumor cell biology laboratory, and Dr. Jack Gruber, formerly of VCP and then NIH, were project officers for the inoculation program. The monkeys were injected with everything from human cancer tissues to rare viruses and even sheep's blood in an effort to find a transmissible cancer. Many of these monkeys succumbed to immunosuppression after infection with the Mason-Pfizer monkey virus, the first known immunosuppressive retrovirus, a class of viruses that includes the human immunodeficiency virus.[31]

Breaking the "Species Barrier"

In 1976, Dr. Seymour Kalter, a prominent NCI scientist and former military medicine expert, reported on experiments so dangerous that other scientists publicly asked for an end to such work.[32] By blending the genetic material of viruses causing cancers in mice and baboons, he created a new virus which could cause cancer in dogs, monkeys, and even chimpanzees. Because it could attack chimpanzees, other scientists feared it could spread to genetically similar human beings. The new virus was a product of some of the first crude genetic "recombination" experiments.

Lawrence Loeb and Kenneth Tartof of the Institute for Cancer Research in Philadelphia, Pennsylvania, went even further in calling for change and called for a ban on such potentially dangerous experimentation.

The production of malignant tumors in a variety of primate species suggests the possibility of creating viruses that are oncogenic for humans... Therefore, we urge that all experiments involving co-cultivation of known oncogenic viruses with primate viruses be immediately halted until the safety of such experiments are [sic] extensively evaluated.[33]

Experiments performed under NCI contract included many dangerous viral inoculation programs, like the primate inoculation program run by Gallo and Gruber. So-called "species barriers" were routinely breached in efforts to find or create infectious cancer viruses. Viruses native to one species were injected into animals from another species in hope of triggering cancers. Often the recipient animal would be immunosuppressed by radiation, drugs, or other treatments. NIH primate researchers were well aware that "the ecological niches of man and animal cross with increasing frequency, and this undoubtedly will create or uncover new disease problems."[34]

At a 1975 NCI symposium, a participant, Dr. J. Moor-Janowski admitted that "environmental-motivated, well-motivated groups begin to consider primate laboratories as being a source of danger." He continued to comment that "a [European] primate center was not able to begin operations as a result of adverse publicity they obtained because of Marburg disease." The speaker was referring to a 1967 outbreak in Yugoslavia and West Germany of this viral disease, which killed several people. Tissues obtained from African Green monkeys used in biomedical work were the source of the mini-epidemic. Dr. Moor-Janowski suggested that researchers should fight against tighter restrictions on primate experiments.[35]

VCP Intellectual Recombination

Under the National Cancer Institute aegis, VCP provided many opportunities for contact between former biological warfare specialists and others in the scientific community. Former biological warfare specialists Drs. Peter Gerone and Arnold Wedum were prominent members of the Biohazard Control and Containment Segment of the VCP. Their positions allowed them frequent contact with laboratories handling hazardous viruses. Gerone and Wedum both worked for many years at Fort Detrick; they were both specialists in the airborne transmission of diseases. In the 1950s, Wedum was in charge of U.S. Army tests of tularemia ("rabbit fever") on human "volunteers." In Gerone's biological warfare research, he used prisoners from the Federal Prison Camp at Eglin Air Force Base in Florida. This group of human guinea pigs was more fortunate than Dr. Wedum's; they were exposed only to cold viruses. Gerone was awarded the army's Meritorious Civilian Service Award for his efforts at Fort Detrick.

The 1975 NCI sponsored symposium on "Biohazards and Zoonotic Problems of Primate Procurement, Quarantine, and Research"[36] illustrates another aspect of NCI-military cooperation. Zoonoses — diseases that can be transmitted from animals to humans — make up the majority of biological warfare agents. The meeting brought together NCI researchers, nine military officers from Major to Lt. Colonel and a civilian from the Edgewood Arsenal, a U.S. chemical warfare facility, also in Maryland. The officers were from the U.S. Army Medical Research Institute of Infectious Diseases, the Defense Nuclear Agency and the Armed Forces Institute of Pathology. In addition, Drs. Wedum, Duff, Gruber, and Gerone were all in attendance.

Gerone presented a paper on the "Biohazards of Experimentally Infected Primates"; he now headed Tulane University's Delta Regional Primate Research Center. In passing, he mentioned aerosol hazards and recommended "exposing animals so that only the head is in contact with the aerosol" rather than using "whole body exposure." Wedum had previously briefed him on biological warfare tests involving just such exposure of monkeys to aerosolized staphy-lococcal enterotoxin; in these tests four Fort Detrick workers still became ill through exposure to the animals. Presumably Gerone was also aware of a 1964 accident when 15 Fort Detrick workers inhaled aerosolized staphylococcal enterotoxin B, "milligram for milligram, one of the most deadly agents ever studied."[37]

In addition to symposia which brought together military and civilian specialists, the VCP utilized consultants with strong biological warfare backgrounds. At times, Dr. Stuart Madin and Mark Chatigny from the NBI, Peter Gerone, and Arthur Brown were all listed as consultants to the NCL. Brown, the former head of the Virus and Rickettsia Division of Fort Detrick, had already been involved in a blatant instance of attempted covert recruitment of microbiologists for biological warfare research.

In 1966, Brown signed a letter soliciting research.[38] It asked scientists to submit proposals to study the recombination of bacteria, but tried to disguise the true source of funding — the Department of Defense. NCI scientist Karl Habel also signed the letter; Habel was "connected with viral research at the National Institutes of Health."[39] The attempt to recruit microbiologists to work on recombination of bacteria fizzled after the funding source was publicly exposed. That it was attempted at all, shows that NIH scientists were willing to team up with the Fort Detrick specialist in covert operations and that some were also willing to deceive their colleagues into collaborating with them.

Coming for Biological Warfare Research

Research into viruses during the War on Cancer provided an ideal cover for continuing biological warfare research. As Colonel Tigertt advised, the NCI project allowed the mass production of viruses, the development of means to enhance virulence, exploration of aerosol transmission, and the production of new recombinant disease agents. These "civilian" projects ran concurrently with "military" projects in many cases. When political expediency dictated an end to overt U.S. Biological warfare research, the Viral Cancer Program provided a means to continue experiments that would otherwise be difficult to justify.

That the United States would covertly continue a biological warfare program should not be quickly discounted. Right up to the start of the VCP, U.S. covert operators conducted clandestine tests simulating aerosol biological weapons attacks. The NBL supplied personnel, lab facilities, and equipment for a secret 1950 aerosol attack on San Francisco, which resulted in dosing almost everyone in the city with a biological warfare agent "simulant."[40] Other secret military experiments used specialized cars and suitcases.[41] The Special Operations Division of the CIA, which operated from Fort Detrick, engaged in similar covert tests using LSD and other chemical agents under the MKULTRA program. Another CIA-SOD program, MKNAOMI, collected biological toxins and disease.[42]

While Nixon ordered a supposed end to biological warfare offensive efforts in 1969, the Central Intelligence Agency retained a secret biological and toxin weapon capability.[43] Given this record of deception in the U.S. biological warfare program, the Viral Cancer Program may well have used the search for a cure for cancer as a cover to continue its experiments on biological warfare.

1991-92

ZIMBABWE'S
ANTHRAX
EPIZOOTIC

Meryl Nass, M.D.

An unusually widespread and sustained epidemic of anthrax spread over Zimbabwe — formerly the British colony of Southern Rhodesia — from 1978 to 1980. It affected large areas, killed thousands of head of livestock, and produced the largest number of human anthrax cases in one disease outbreak ever reported in the world. It caused extensive economic hardship in areas with a predominantly black population, while leaving white areas unscathed. Was it bad luck or biological warfare?

The epidemic coincided with civil war in Zimbabwe.[1] During the 1960s, Britain was granting independence and majority (*i.e.*, black) rule to its African colonies. As a means of ensuring continued white domination of the country, the Rhodesian white minority, under Ian

Smith, preemptively declared independence from Britain in 1965. A small black guerrilla movement started and gradually enlarged, with the assistance of other nations, into a war.

As the war escalated, the government enacted increasingly harsh measures to punish any rural blacks it suspected of supporting the guerrillas. These actions further polarized the population.[2] The whites — less than 10 percent of the population — began to realize that despite the use of mercenaries and black African soldiers, they lacked the manpower to win a guerrilla war.

In this setting of escalating war, terrorism, and random violence, the black population experienced an increase in human and animal disease. Given that medical and veterinary services in the rural areas had become almost nonexistent as the war progressed, this rise did not seem too surprising. Anthrax was one of the diseases which experienced an upsurge toward the end of the war.[3]

Anthrax had been present for a long time in Zimbabwe, as in most other countries, but Zimbabwe had historically experienced only a small number of cases. In fact, in 1967, it had been designated in the lowest incidence category for countries with anthrax.[4] All this changed at the end of 1978, when a major outbreak of anthrax began, and then spread throughout many regions of the country. "By the end of 1979, it [anthrax] was estimated to be active in about one third of the tribal areas of the country."[5]

Unusual Features of the Epizootic

In order to explore whether Zimbabwe's anthrax epizootic (a disease outbreak affecting more than one species) was a natural occurrence, it is necessary to determine if the properties of the epizootic were compatible with the known behavior of anthrax in nature. It is also important to examine carefully all the hypotheses that have been proposed to explain the unusual characteristics of the epizootic, to see whether or not they can provide a convincing rationale for the observed behavior. Although the second type of detailed analysis is beyond the scope of the present article, it is available elsewhere.[6]

Number of Cases: The anthrax epizootic exhibited a number of peculiar features. First, the large number of cases was in itself unusual. An average of only 13 human cases a year had been reported in Zimbabwe prior to the onset of the epizootic. Yet from 1979 through 1980, 10,738 human cases were documented and 182 people died of anthrax.[7] "At the beginning of what was to be a major epidemic," wrote Zimbabwean physician J.C.A. Davies, who wrote extensively about the epizootic, "it is safe to say that the majority of doctors in Zimbabwe had never seen a case of anthrax."[8]

Unusually Wide Area and Long Duration: In Zimbabwe, the disease spread over time from area to area, into six of the eight provinces.[9] Yet, in the rest of the world, anthrax is considered to be a disease that is endemic in certain areas only. Those areas where the anthrax organisms can undergo the vegetative phase of their life cycle, multiply, and then resporulate (reproduce) are limited. The soil must have an alkaline pH, and contain sufficient nitrogen, calcium, and organic matter. Based on epidemiologic analysis of anthrax outbreaks, it appears that extreme weather conditions must be present as well, in order for anthrax to compete successfully with the other microorganisms present in soil. A drought followed by heavy rains is an example of a weather pattern which has often preceded anthrax outbreaks.

Sufficiently high soil concentrations of anthrax spores to cause disease in animals who ingest them, seem to be sustained only transiently. Epizootics, therefore, usually only last for periods of weeks, and occur only in limited areas. There is no significant spread from animal to animal. Humans generally acquire the disease from contact with infected animal products, and there is little if any human to human spread. Therefore, anthrax epizootics do not spread to distant areas, and tend to resemble "point source" outbreaks of disease, such as food poisoning epidemics, rather than epidemics of diseases which spread by contagion, such as chicken pox.

Unusual Pattern of Distribution: Many of the Zimbabwean cases occurred in areas where anthrax had not previously been reported. Yet in the rest of the world, epizootics generally occur in areas known to have produced anthrax outbreaks in the past, where there is assumed to be chronic low density contamination of the soil. (Anthrax spores in soil may retain their virulence for decades.) The disease does not spread outside these areas. The exception to this occurs when an area has become newly contaminated. For example, use of bone meal fertilizer made from infected animals and found to contain anthrax spores has caused outbreaks in England. However, fertilizers made from animal remains were not commonly used in the affected areas of Zimbabwe.[10]

Confined to National Borders: One would have thought that if weather conditions particularly favored the growth of anthrax in many areas throughout Zimbabwe, and often near its borders, then other anthrax outbreaks in adjoining countries would have occurred as well. Yet there were no reports of increased anthrax activity elsewhere in the region.[11]

Respected Race of Inhabitants: The epizootic was almost entirely confined to the black farming areas and black population; the 50 percent of Zimbabwe's land used by white commercial farmers was essentially unaffected. According to Zimbabwe Research Laboratory scientists, by early 1980 only four anthrax outbreaks, with 11 associated cattle deaths, had been reported in the commercial (white-owned) farming areas, while thousands of cases had occurred in the communal (black) farming areas.[12]

Significant Timing: The epizootic coincided with the final months of a long, brutal guerrilla war, which pitted black against white, and trailed off after the end of the war.

Evidence of Biological Warfare

For this outbreak to have been a biological warfare event, both anthrax spores and delivery systems would have had to be available to a perpetrator. Given the fairly large land areas involved, were means of dissemination available that could have produced an epizootic of anthrax in cattle and cutaneous anthrax in humans, comparable to that which occurred? Could spreading a disease to animals and/or humans conceivably have aided the war effort?

There is evidence that obtaining or producing spores was within the means of those countries that wanted them. Production of spores is not technically difficult. Japan, the United Kingdom, and the United States produced them as long as 50 years ago.[13] The United States is known to have created and stored such weapons until they were destroyed following Nixon's 1969 ban. A number of biological weapons was found in a CIA freezer after all U.S. biological weapons were reported to have been destroyed, ostensibly stored by a CIA employee without higher approval.[14]

Given the scope of foreign involvement with Rhodesia, the white government may have received the weapons from a country which had a secret program. It is also possible that Rhodesia was able to produce such materials domestically. Many delivery systems for anthrax spores are relatively simple to produce or procure.[15] They could have allowed for the careful demarcation between affected and unaffected areas which was exhibited by the Zimbabwe epizootic. The simplest method of dissemination would have been by air, but other methods for contaminating the soil were also possible.

As to the utility of the epidemic, it is reasonable to ask how a disease that killed primarily cows, and usually produced curable skin ulcers in people, could be useful to the Rhodesian Government's war effort. A review of some of the actions and strategies used by Rhodesia's military sheds light on this question. It indicates the range of military actions that was performed, and thus, considered acceptable.

Although in the early years of the conflict the guerrillas tended to engage in independent actions and remain in isolated areas, they soon learned that the political and material support of the indigenous peoples was essential to their success. They began regular nighttime meetings with local populations for political and historical education. People who had been initially willing to inform on strangers began to find reasons to support the insurgent cause. Both the government forces and the guerrillas began to seek out and punish those who betrayed them. As the war intensified and government administrative and educational systems broke down or were driven out, the guerrillas replaced them with their own institutions. Rhodesian military strategists knew that it was essential to separate the rural peasants from the guerrillas. Lt. Col. I. Bates listed some of the military's counterinsurgency tactics used in northeast Rhodesia in 1974:

> Large external operations [attacks on neighboring countries] to turn off the tap [of insurgents re-entering the country]; a *cordon*

sanitaire with warning devices, patrolled and backed by a 20 km.-wide no-go area; population control consisting of Protected Villages, food con-trol, curfews, and (eventually) martial law.[16]

The Consequences of the Epidemic

As the war dragged on, many Rhodesian whites left the country and, eventually, all remaining white males from 18 to 58 years old were drafted to perform some military duty. Meanwhile, the economy came to a standstill and the Rhodesian Government grew desperate. Despite imposing harsh measures including martial law, it was no closer to winning the war.

Under these circumstances, an epidemic such as anthrax would have further reduced the wealth and food supply of the rural people. The loss of cattle was a particularly critical problem for Rhodesia's rural blacks. There is always hardship, but if cattle die, the family loses its source of wealth; without motive power for plowing, crops cannot be planted leading to no food, no money to purchase food, pay school fees, bus fares, taxes, or buy the essentials to life. The family is reduced to grinding poverty, and malnutrition becomes rife.[17]

A second effect of the anthrax outbreak might have been the confusion and fear generated by the appearance of an epidemic which affected only rural people and their cattle, particularly in areas of heavy guerrilla activity, yet spared whites. Certainly attempts had been made to exploit other events, such as droughts, as a sign of displeasure from the spirits. It is not inconceivable that the effects of anthrax and of organophosphates were put to this purpose as well.

In any event, large-scale bombing raids into neighboring Mozambique and Zambia, use of organophosphates, the tactics employed by the Selous Scouts, provide examples of the Rhodesian military's disregard for the lives of black civilians.

Furthermore, Zimbabwe faced no international legal impediment against use of such weapons. Although the United Kingdom was a party to the Geneva Protocol, which banned the use of chemical and bacteriological agents in war, Rhodesia had declared its independence from Britain in 1965; thus Rhodesia was probably not subject to the Geneva Protocol.

Legal Constraints on Biological Weaponry

The 1925 Geneva Protocol had banned chemical and bacteriological agents in war. It was provoked by widespread revulsion against the chemical weapons which had caused about 100,000 deaths and over 1 million casualties in World War I.

Although it outlawed wartime use, the protocol did not ban development, production, possession, or use outside wartime. Nor did it establish investigatory or sanctioning mechanisms in the case of violation.[18] Many nations reserved the right to retaliatory use, only giving up *first use*. Even within these limited constraints, becoming a party to the convention did not guarantee compliance. In 1936, Italy, which *had* signed and ratified the treaty, sprayed Ethiopia with mustard gas, killing 15,000 soldiers and civilians.

The United States signed but never ratified the treaty; during World War II, in conjunction with Great Britain, it began a biological warfare program, focused on the development of anthrax and botulism weapons.[19] After the war, the decision was made to continue the program.

The 1975 Biological Weapons Convention was a much more comprehensive treaty than the Geneva Protocol in that, in addition to use, it banned research, development, production, and possession of biological weapons or toxins for offensive use. It did, however, allow countries to retain stores of biological (weapons) agents necessary for "prophylactic or peaceful purposes." No precise definition of this wording appears in the treaty, nor are acceptable quantities of microorganisms specified. National Security Decision Memorandum 35, signed by Nixon's National Security Adviser, Henry Kissinger, and issued on the same day as Nixon's renunciation of biological weapons, specifically defined as permissible "research into those offensive aspects of... biological agents necessary to determine what defensive measures are required."[20] The corollary suggests offensive agents may be produced so that defenses against them can be tested.

Although the 1975 treaty specifies that parties must enact "enabling" domestic legislation to enforce treaty provisions within member countries, compliance with this provision has lagged. The U.S. Congress, for instance, waited 14 years, until 1989, to pass legislation criminalizing the production and possession of biological weapons. Furthermore, the treaty itself carries no provisions for verification of compliance or sanctions for violators.

Preventing Biological Warfare

As we have seen, treaties alone do not stop biological warfare. Biological weapons are clearly "useful," and serve best as covert agents. Secrecy not only adds to the element of terror, but also generally guarantees anonymity and the absence of reprisals to a perpetrator. Biological warfare usually spares property, harming only crops, animals, or people, depending on the agent(s) selected for use. It fits particularly well with civil war, "low-intensity conflict," special operations, counterinsurgency, and assassinations. Historically, biological weapons have been used by the technologically more advanced against the less developed, since countries with extensive public and animal health infrastructures are difficult to harm seriously and are more likely to detect an attack.

Given this utility, the failure of treaties,[21] and the long history of biological warfare (dating back at least to the 14th century when plague-infected bodies were thrown over the city walls to infect the besieged Black Sea port of Caffa), how can this form of warfare be prevented?

Thus far, no allegation of biological warfare has been scientifically investigated and conclusively resolved. Researchers must begin by analyzing epidemics with unusual epidemiology, as was done here for Zimbabwe. No nongovernmental organization or international agency is doing epidemic surveillance for possible biological weapons. Although military agencies are charged with performing this function, their methods and results are classified and therefore unavailable to the international community.

A strong international body should be empowered and funded to investigate thoroughly, draw conclusions, seek out, and punish perpetrators of biological warfare actions. The United States, however, has recently obstructed the Biological Weapons Convention Third Review Conference (the international body with the mission of improving the Biological Weapons Convention effectiveness) from developing effective measures for verification and compliance.[22]

Biological warfare is a human rights issue. To expose human

beings deliberately to disease is not only a violation of international laws, it is immoral. The purpose for using biological warfare on domestic animals and crops can only be to create famine. Thus, hunger and disease become primary weapons of war. Only the refusal of informed citizens to tolerate the existence of biological weapons will force governments, which value expedience above morality, to cease their use.

1992-93

U.S. BIOLOGICAL WARFARE:

THE 1981 CUBA DENGUE

EPIDEMIC

William H. Schaap

For more than 20 years Cuba has been the victim of American attacks, overt and covert, large and small, unrelenting. Ships and buildings have been bombed; cane fields have been burned; invasions have been launched; and planes have been blown out of the sky. But many of the attacks have been even less conventional. Cuba has seen its share of chemical-biological warfare — some of which has been proved, some of which has not. If the Cuban charges are true — and we believe that this article will help demonstrate that they are — then the dengue fever epidemic of 1981 was only the latest in a long line of outrageous, immoral, and illegal chemical-biological warfare attacks against Cuba.[1]

The History of Attacks

Many studies have been written on the chemical-biological warfare capabilities of the United States. Some have discussed specifics; some have mentioned Cuba. John Marks, Victor Marchetti, Philip Agee, and Seymour Hersh have all discussed various specifics. Shortly after the triumph of the Cuban Revolution, during the early 1960s, food poisoning attempts were common, often at the same time that crop burnings were being carried out. A *Washington Post* report (September 16, 1977) confirmed that during this time the CIA maintained an "anti-crop warfare" program. Both the CIA and the army were studying biological warfare, primarily at the facilities of Fort Detrick, Maryland. Dr. Marc Lappe noted in his book, *Chemical and Biological Warfare: The Science of Public Death*, that the army had a biological warfare agent prepared for use against Cuba at the time of the Missile Crisis in 1962; it was most likely Q fever.

Throughout the 1960s there were occasional biological attacks against Cuba, sometimes, according to Cuban allegations in 1964, involving apparent weather balloons. And in 1970 the CIA engineered the introduction of African swine fever into Cuba, a successful operation carried out by Cuban exile agents.[2] It led to the forced destruction of more than a half million pigs. The same groups attempted unsuccessfully a few months later to infect the Cuban poultry industry. These operations were first exposed in *Newsday* (January 9, 1977), and later appeared in the *Washington Post*, *Le Monde*, the *Guardian*, and other papers.

Then, in 1980 — the year of the plagues — Cuba was beset with disasters. Another African swine fever epidemic hit; the tobacco crop was decimated by blue mold; and the sugarcane crops were hit with a particularly damaging rust disease. As *The Nation* put it, this was "a conjunction of plagues that would lead people less paranoid about the United States than the Cubans to wonder whether human hands had played a role in these natural disasters..."

It is against this backdrop that the Cubans found themselves facing, in the spring and summer of 1981, an unprecedented epidemic of hemorrhagic dengue fever.

Why Dengue?

As noted above, the arsenal of chemical-biological warfare is unlimited. The U.S. military and the CIA have experimented with diseases which merely make a person uncomfortable for a few hours, with toxins which kill instantly, and with everything in between. John Marks describes a few in his study of MKULTRA, the CIA's mind control experiment, *The Search for the "Manchurian Candidate."* Staphylococcal enterotoxin, for example, a mild food poisoning, would incapacitate its victim for three to six hours; Venezuelan equine encephalomyelitis (VEE) virus would immobilize a person for two to five days and keep its victims weak for perhaps another month; brucellosis would keep its victims in the hospital for three or more months, killing some. Even the deadly poisons were prepared with variations: shellfish toxin kills within a few seconds; botulinum, however, takes eight to 12 hours, giving the assassin time to get away.

Dengue fever is one of some 250 arthropod-borne viruses, or "arboviruses," diseases transmitted from one vertebrate to another by hematophagous arthropods — blood eating insects, usually mosquitoes. Dengue is transmitted by the *Aedes aegypti* mosquito, the same insect which transmits yellow fever. There are four types of dengue, numbered one through four, depending on the type of antibody which the virus induces. Normal dengue fever begins with the same symptoms as a severe cold or flu, watery eyes, runny nose, headache, backache, fever, insomnia, lack of appetite, and weakness. The bone pain is incapacitating. Indeed, dengue was once known as "break bone." Its characteristic symptom is pain at the back of the eyes, most noticeable when looking from side to side. All types of dengue can give rise to the hemorrhagic form, that is, accompanied by internal bleeding and shock. This form is the most dangerous, especially to children, for whom it is often fatal.

Dengue and other arboviruses are ideal as biological warfare weapons for a number of reasons. Dengue, especially hemorrhagic dengue, is highly incapacitating; it can be transmitted easily through the introduction of infected mosquitoes; it will spread rapidly, especially in highly populated and damp areas. The *Aedes* mosquito bites during the day, when people are more active and less protected; moreover, in favorable winds, *Aedes* mosquitoes can travel hundreds of miles before landing, none the worse for wear. And, of course, since dengue fever is found in nature in many parts of the world, a human role in its spread is hard to detect. This is the inherent advantage of biological over chemical warfare.

The 1981 Epidemic

Although dengue fever is much more common in the Far East, there have been many outbreaks in the Caribbean and Central America during the past century. All four types have been found during the last two decades. In 1963 there was a dengue-3 outbreak in Puerto Rico and Antigua; in 1968, dengue-2 was found in Jamaica; in 1977, dengue-1 was found in Jamaica and Cuba; and in 1981, dengue-4 was found in the Lesser Antilles.

The epidemic which hit Cuba in May 1981 was of type 2 dengue with hemorrhagic shock. Except for the type 1 epidemic reported in 1977, this was the first major dengue outbreak in Cuba since 1944, and, most importantly, the first in the Caribbean since the turn of the century to involve hemorrhagic shock on a massive scale.

From May to October 1981 there were well over 300,000 reported cases, with 158 fatalities, 101 involving children under 15. At the peak of the epidemic, in early July, more than 10,000 cases per day were being reported. More than a third of the reported victims required hospitalization. By mid-October, after a massive campaign to eradicate *Aedes aegypti*, the epidemic was over.

The history of the secret war against Cuba and the virulence of this dengue epidemic were enough to generate serious suspicions that the United States had a hand in the dengue epidemic of 1981. But there is much more support for those suspicions than a healthy distrust of U.S. intentions regarding Cuba.

The Clues

We reviewed the reports on the epidemic of the Pan American Health Organization and of the Cuban Ministry of Public Health, and interviewed a number of health officials. There are indeed indications that the epidemic was artificially induced.

The epidemic began with the simultaneous discovery in May 1981 of three cases of hemorrhagic dengue caused by a type 2 virus. The cases arose in three widely separated parts of Cuba: Cienfuegos, Camagüey, and Havana. It is extremely unusual that such an epidemic would commence in three different localities at once. None of the initial victims had ever traveled out of the country; for that matter, none of them had recently been away from home. None had had recent contact with international travelers. Moreover, a study of persons arriving in Cuba in the month of May from known dengue areas found only a dozen such passengers (from Vietnam and Laos), all of whom were checked by the Institute of Tropical Medicine and found free of the disease. Somehow, infected mosquitoes had appeared in three provinces of Cuba at the same time. Somehow, the fever spread at an astonishing rate. There appears to be no other explanation but the artificial introduction of infected mosquitoes.

Another, less sinister conclusion might be possible if there were epidemics raging in neighboring islands. But, on the contrary, there were no epidemics taking place elsewhere in the Caribbean. Statistics published by the Pan American Health Organization show that during the first eight months of 1981, when there were over 300,000 cases of dengue in Cuba, there were no cases reported in Jamaica, none in the Bahamas, and only 22 in Haiti. In all the rest of the Caribbean and Central America, there were less than 6,000 cases of dengue, half of them in Colombia. And, most significantly, only in Cuba were the cases mostly hemorrhagic.

Weather Modification?

Yet another peculiarity involves the unprecedented rainfall throughout much of Cuba during the winter and spring preceding the epidemic. This led to an unusual accumulation of mosquito breeding areas, which undoubtedly helped the spread of the dengue once infected insects arrived. Statistics for the three provinces in which the epidemic began show that rainfall in March, for example, was double the average. Similar statistics prevailed in more than half the provinces of the country.

Whether this unusual precipitation was the result of artificial weather modification coordinated with the release of infected *Aedes* mosquitoes or merely a fortuitous coincidence taken advantage of by the planners of this action is not provable at this time. It is clear though that the increase in precipitation was dramatic, and it is well known that the United States has been involved in weather modification for many years. It is known that cloud seeding was used in the Vietnam War in an attempt to cause the weakening of dikes and the flooding of rice fields. But it has also been noted that Cuba was the victim of weather modification.

"During 1969 and 1970," according to Hinckle and Turner, "the CIA deployed futuristic weather modification technology to ravage Cuba's sugar crop and undermine the economy. Planes from the China Lake Naval Weapons Center in the California desert, where hi-tech was developed, overflew the island, seeding rain clouds with crystals that precipitated torrential rains over nonagricultural areas and left the cane fields arid (the downpours caused killer flash floods in some areas)."

If that kind of pinpoint accuracy was possible, and Hinckle and Turner got their information from participants, then preparing the breeding grounds for mosquitoes would be a simple task.

Arbovirus Research

Most important, perhaps, is U.S. familiarity with arbovirus transmission, with years of biological warfare research involving *Aedes* and other mosquitoes and dengue and other fevers. As has been documented in Seymour Hersh's *Chemical and Biological Warfare: America's Hidden Arsenal*, the United States has been experimenting with dengue fever since at least 1959, primarily at Fort Detrick in Maryland and at Walter Reed Army Institute of Research in Washington. Public reports as early as 1963 (*e.g.*, *Military Medicine*, February 1963) stressed a need for research into arbovirus biological warfare. Of course, these early public reports did not point out that such research was already taking place. Also, there are reports that as early as 1972 U.S. researchers were working on possible vaccines against type 2 dengue.

A review of publicly available summaries of research projects confirms the government's open sponsorship of extensive research into dengue fever and related diseases for many years. Dozens of these projects, costing millions of dollars, have been funded by the Department of Defense. The justifications stated are, of course, defensive; "essential in formulating preventive measures for the protection of ground forces if committed to those areas" is how one summary puts it. But the public summaries recognize that arboviruses may be used in biological warfare. One notes that research into the debilitating effects of dengue fever is necessary not only to protect against "natural threats to U.S. forces in various parts of the world," but also because they are diseases "against which medical defenses will be required should they be used as biological agents." All the reports suggest that the United States wants to know about chemical-biological warfare only for defensive purposes — because others might use it against the United States. Therein lies the difficulty in fighting the chemical-biological warfare trend. Research for "defensive" purposes and research for "offensive" purposes are indistinguishable.

The connections between the academic community and the government, especially the military, are pervasive. Nearly all the leading researchers have been connected intimately with military investigations into chemical-biological warfare.

One leading scientist in this field is Dr. Charles Calisher, an arbovirus expert for the Pan American Health Organization (PAHO), a division of the World Health Organization. Since 1971 Dr. Calisher has worked at the Fort Collins laboratories of the U.S. Centers for Disease Control in Georgia. Dr. Calisher has of late been viewed with extreme suspicion by Cuban health officials. As noted above, from 1944 to 1977 there was virtually no dengue in Cuba; nevertheless, health officials were always concerned about arboviruses because of the prevalence of mosquitoes. In 1972 Cuban health officials began a serious study of dengue, including attendance at PAHO meetings. At a 1974 meeting Calisher made many inquiries about dengue in Cuba and expressed a strong desire to visit and study the arbovirus situation in Cuba. In 1975 he visited the island; according to Cuban sources Dr. Calisher predicted at that time that Cuba might face a dengue epidemic within two years, because, he said, of their relations with Africa. Then, in 1977, for the first time in 33 years, there was a dengue epidemic in Cuba.

When Cuban officials charged that the 1981 epidemic was a clandestine operation of the United States, Dr. Calisher was one of the U.S. experts who publicly belittled the accusation, pointing out that there were many mosquitoes on Cuba, and stressing its relations with nations of Africa and Southeast Asia. This explanation was given even though, as noted above, visitors from dengue areas had been checked and even though the initial cases were unrelated to foreign travel.

Another of the most active researchers today is Dr. William F. Scherer of Cornell University. According to his entry in *Who's Who*, from 1965 to 1972 he directed the viral infection committee of the Armed Forces Epidemiology Board. Dr. Scherer has directed a number of projects, often with Department of Defense funding, studying arbovirus vectors — that is, the hosts that transmit the viruses from one victim to another. These studies, in which he has been engaged since 1972, have covered the use as vectors of various species of mosquitoes and, in addition, birds and bats.

Defense Department arbovirus research is still going on. On February 17, 1982, the Under Secretary of Defense for Research and Engineering delivered to the Senate a required report on "funds obligated in the chemical warfare and biological defense research programs during FY 1981." (The term "biological defense" is always used even though there is virtually no difference between biological offense and biological defense research. This is in large part because a 1972 treaty to which the United States is a party outlaws biological warfare research, development, or stockpiling, *except* for defensive research.) The report noted nearly $12 million was obligated to "risk assessment and evaluation of viral agents and their vectors that pose a biological warfare threat." The studies included investigations into the "growth and survival" of various arboviruses in mosquitoes, "new techniques" for infecting mosquitoes with hemorrhagic fevers, and other such "defensive" research.

Conclusions

That the dengue epidemic *could* have been a covert U.S. operation is clear. It is a plausible hypothesis, consistent with past actions. Moreover, there is ample evidence that the United States has been investigating the biological warfare possibilities of dengue fever for many years. And it is U.S. experimentation which has shown that *Aedes aegypti* mosquitoes (infected with dengue) could travel hundreds of miles, along the path of the prevailing winds, from the place of release to the place of landing. A boat off the coast of Florida at the right time with the right winds could sprinkle mosquitoes on Cuba with no fear of infecting the mainland. Of course, it is also possible that a ship or plane based at Guantánamo could have been used.

That the epidemic *was* an American covert action is less easily demonstrated, but there are many indications that this is true, and that the Cuban accusation is valid. The most significant fact is the simultaneous outbreak of the disease in three widely separated locations. When one confirms that these first three cases did not involve foreign travel or contact with foreign travelers, and one confirms that the people who arrived in Cuba from dengue infected areas during the several weeks preceding the outbreak were not infected, the only logical conclusion is the artificial introduction of the disease. Moreover, there were no epidemics in nearby countries. In addition, this was the first time in the Caribbean in this century that an epidemic of this size involved hemorrhagic shock, the most dangerous form of dengue fever. Dengue fever, as a biological weapon, would undoubtedly be of the hemorrhagic form.

And, finally, there is the unusual precipitation shortly before the outbreak of the epidemic. For such an operation to be successful, it would be necessary to ensure a very large mosquito population at the time of the introduction of the infected vectors; otherwise the rapid and devastating spread of the disease would not be guaranteed.

Perhaps some day the full truth will be known. But for those who have studied the recent history of the United States, for those who know of what it is capable, for those who see the absence of any morality in the vicious, uninterrupted 23-year campaign against Cuba, for them there is no justification whatsoever to give the United States the benefit of the doubt.

Afterword: Omega 7 and Dengue Fever

For over a month Eduardo Victor Arocena Perez was on trial in the Federal District Court for the Southern District of New York. He was accused of being "Omar," the notorious head of the Cuban exile terrorist organization Omega 7, and was charged with the 1980 murder of Félix García Rodríguez, an attaché at the Cuban Mission to the United Nations, along with nearly two dozen other crimes. On September 22, 1984, he was found guilty of all but one minor charge.

What is of more than passing interest is a portion of his testimony in his own defense. The transcript (pp. 2187-2189) for September 10, 1984, reads in pertinent part as follows:

> Q: Did there come a time in 1980 when you moved your family to Miami, Florida?
>
> A: It was the latter part. We did move to Miami. It was toward the end of 1980...
>
> Q: In 1980, sir, did you participate in the Mariel boat lift?
>
> A: Yes, sir.
>
> Q: What was your involvement in the Mariel boat lift, sir?
>
> A: I had two objectives. One was to get in touch with my family, and the other was to make contact with the insurrectionists inside Cuba, to supervise an action that was being carried out at that time inside Cuban territory.
>
> Q: Did you travel to Cuba, sir?
>
> A: Yes, sir.
>
> Q: Whom did you meet in Cuba?
>
> A: With several high officials of the regime in Cuba, military.
>
> Q: What regime is this, sir?
>
> A: The communist regime of Cuba.
>
> Q: Sir, weren't you fighting – I am sorry...
>
> A: But I clarify this, that these officials are part of the resistance. Part of the objective was that before me, ahead of me was another ship with a different mission, a mission that was to be carried out inside Cuban territory, as I stated before... The group that was ahead of me had a mission to carry some germs to introduce them in Cuba to be used against the Soviets and against the Cuban economy, to begin what was called chemical war, which later on produced results that were not what we had expected, because we thought that it was going to be used against the Soviet forces, and it was used against our own people, and with that we did not agree.

The implications of this information are very significant, indicating that in late 1980 or early 1981 a virulent strain of dengue fever was introduced into Cuba in a biological warfare operation.

It now seems clear from Arocena's testimony that Omega 7 agents were doing the dirty work for the CIA and the U.S. Government. Why he thought it would be to his benefit to testify about a part in a biological warfare operation is hard to explain, but this is not the first time the villains have provided proof of their own villainy.

1982, 1984

AGENT ORANGE:
THE DIRTY LEGAL
WAR AT HOME

A. Namika

On May 7, 1984, nine years after the Vietnam War ended and six years after the first Agent Orange claim was filed in New York State, Judge Jack B. Weinstein of the Federal District Court in the Eastern District of New York "settled" the case. The chemical companies which had manufactured the deadly dioxin-laden herbicide used to defoliate Vietnam were pleased with the decision. The thousands of veterans who were ill, or dying, or had children with birth defects, however, felt that they had been denied justice. They charged that the federal courts helped the chemical companies avoid paying billions of dollars to those injured in the Dirty War.[1]

The Agent Orange Cover-Up

Another six years later, a 1990 congressional investigation revealed that the Reagan-Bush administrations had manipulated a Centers for Disease Control (CDC) study on the effects of the toxins.[2] Initiated in 1982, the controversial CDC study of Agent Orange exposure and Vietnam veterans' health was terminated in 1987 after concluding that damage from the herbicide could not be assessed. Pressured by veterans' groups, the Human Resources and Intergovernmental Relations Subcommittee (HRIRS) conducted a year-long (1989-90) exhaustive investigation into the CDC study.

The HRIRS subcommittee found that the Agent Orange exposure study should not have been cancelled. CDC's inability to assess exposure and correlate it with illness resulted from a flawed investigation, not a lack of evidence. "Other methods were available," charged the subcommittee, "but [were] intentionally disregarded." The report concluded that "the CDC study was changed from its original format so that it would have been unlikely for the soldiers who received the heaviest exposure to the herbicide to be identified."[3]

The subcommittee also concluded that the CDC study was controlled and obstructed by the White House, primarily through its Agent Orange Working Group (AOWG) and the Office of Management and Budget (OMB), "because the Reagan administration had adopted a legal strategy of refusing liability in military and civilian cases of contamination involving toxic chemicals and nuclear radiation."[4]

With the government absolved by its legal immunity from responsibility for injuries to military personnel, the veterans' only recourse was to sue the chemical companies for damages. At about the same time as the initiation and eventual subversion of the CDC study, the first Agent Orange suit was winding its way through the courts. Judge Weinstein, who took over the case in 1983, rejected the plaintiffs' expert witnesses. He was, however, open to "scientific" evidence provided by the very chemical companies that had produced the deadly herbicide and ruled that there was no evidence that the toxin had injured anyone.

A number of Agent Orange cases had been filed against chemical companies in the late 1970s when increasing numbers of Vietnam vets began dying prematurely, reporting debilitating illnesses, or claiming their children had birth defects. Most of these cases were consolidated into a class action, *Ryan v. Dow*, in the Eastern District Court of New York.

When the ostensibly liberal Judge Weinstein "contrived" a settlement,[5] the named chemical companies – including Monsanto Co., Hercules Co. Inc., T.H. Agriculture & Nutrition Co. Inc., Diamond Shamrock Chemicals Co., Uniroyal, Inc., and Thompson Chemicals Corporation, as well as Dow Chemical Co. – were gleeful. Their stocks registered an immediate gain on the New York Stock Exchange.[6] The reaction of the veterans, however, was almost overwhelmingly negative.

In 1989, some veterans and their relatives – who had not experienced any dioxin-related illnesses at the time of the first settlement, and therefore did not consider themselves bound by it – filed a second Agent Orange case in Texas. On request of the defendant chemical companies, the Multi-District Litigation (MDL) panel, appointed by Chief Justice William Rehnquist, removed *Ivy v. Diamond Shamrock* to the same Brooklyn judge who had forced the meager settlement in the first case. The vets subsequently asked Weinstein to withdraw, charging that the judge had a conflict of interest because of his fiduciary role in a foundation he had established using the funds from the 1984 settlement. If *Ivy* were returned to Texas, the fund would lose $10 million.

A Judge's Fiefdom

In the earlier case, the court had rejected expert evidence from the vets connecting Agent Orange to the host of cancers and neurological diseases which afflicted them. By the time of the *Ivy* case, the link had been irrefutably established. Instead of barring the new evidence, Weinstein did the next best thing – he discounted its relevance.[7] He handed down novel decisions leading finally to his April 1992 dismissal of the case solely on procedural grounds. *Ivy* is now on appeal in the Second Circuit.

At first glance, Weinstein's original 1984 settlement of Agent Orange class action litigation seemed to favor the veterans. The $180 million figure was the largest amount of damages recovered in any personal injury suit. Nonetheless, most of the 2,500 veteran plaintiffs who spoke at "fairness hearings" held by the judge, came away feeling ignored and bitter.[8] The judge had divided the settlement into two separate funds. One delivered an average $3,200 for death and total disability claims, and nothing for any lesser injuries.[9]

"By contrast, [when *Ivy* was filed] more than $20 million had already gone to the plaintiffs' lawyers, court-appointed officials, retained experts, and the company that administers the veterans' claims, court records show."[10]

The second fund, the $52 million Agent Orange Class Assistance Program (AOCAP), is basically a grant-making foundation under Weinstein's direct supervision and control, administered by managers whom he hires. In a 1991 "guidance" memo, grantees were issued a virtual gag order on the day Weinstein decided the *Ivy* case: "Speaking as AOCAP-funded program representatives, you may not take a position on the case or Judge Weinstein's ruling. Nor may you express opinions as to the causal relationship between Agent Orange and any specific ailment or condition."[11]

The later case, *Ivy, et al.*, argues that Weinstein, in effect, created a virtual fiefdom, using the settlement money to control veterans' organizations and influence government policy.[12] The brief also asserts that the judge has influenced the advocacy efforts of the veterans' leadership and redirected its attention from issues adversely affecting the interests of Agent Orange manufacturers, who would, were it not for Weinstein's intervention, face billions of dollars of potential liabilities.[13]

If veterans or their families, who were not involved in the 1984 settlement, accept any assistance from either fund, they risk sacrificing future claims against the chemical companies and having the settlement retroactively enforced on them.

This forfeiture includes the genetically damaged children of Vietnam veterans, many of whom were not even born at the time of the settlement.

Media-Industry Blitz on Dioxin

In the wake of damaging evidence from the *Ivy* case and several other court struggles on the effects of dioxin (a major toxin in Agent Orange), chemical companies began an orchestrated media blitz. In 1990, Dr.

Vernon Houk, who had been senior statistician in the Agent Orange CDC study, asserted that previous assessments of the harmful effects of dioxin were overestimated. Since 1983, he claimed "there has been a large body of human data accumulated that indicated, in my opinion, that man is not as susceptible to the consequences of dioxin exposure as many of the animal species studied to date."[14] When cross-examined by late Congressmember Ted Weiss (Dem.-N.Y.) in his subcommittee hearings, Houk admitted contact with the paper industry while he was developing new relaxed standards of dioxin exposure.[15] The chemical and paper industries quickly took up Houk's refrain that dioxin was less toxic than previously believed.[16]

Admiral Elmo Zumwalt, commander of U.S. naval forces in Vietnam (1968-70) and member of the Joint Chiefs of Staff (1970-74) became an ally of the vets after his son died of Agent Orange-related causes. He charged that Houk's widely quoted statements were "politically motivated efforts to cover up the true effects of dioxin, and manipulate public perception [and] coincide with similar, economically motivated, efforts of chemical companies that produce dioxin."[17]

Congressmember Ted Weiss, whose subcommittee spearheaded the Agent Orange investigation was alarmed by the PR campaign. "Dioxin," he said, "is unsafe at any dose. The public has been duped by an industry propaganda campaign and a handful of federal scientists who have carried the industry's message to the highest levels of government. They have spread false information about new scientific evidence that dioxin is safe at low levels, and that federal standards should be weakened."[18]

Implications for Other Mass Toxic Tort Cases

The Agent Orange case has established precedents for "settling" cases so that chemical companies and other corporate criminals get off relatively cheaply – *i.e.*, for hundreds of millions rather than the billions of dollars that could result from a jury verdict. Under Weinstein's approach, a mass toxic tort settlement can put a federal judge in control of a small financial empire on behalf of an ill-defined and powerless constituency of injured plaintiffs. At present, the dockets of the state and federal courts are "swamped" with tort claims over exposure to radiation, formaldehyde, benzene, lead, silicone, DES, and bendectin, as chemical companies and their lawyers point out.[19] For asbestos products alone, in 1991, there were about 100,000 pending claims in the federal and state court systems.

The solution recommended by corporations facing mass toxic tort cases such as Agent Orange, Bhopal, asbestos, etc., is to prevent them from ever reaching a jury. Under the guise of cutting litigation costs, corporate law firms try to tailor "designer settlements," like that for the 1989 Agent Orange case, for use in the event of any disaster. The Center for Claims Resolution (CCR), which has endorsed such settlements in an *amicus* brief in support of defendants in the *Ivy* case, is a non-profit organization, formed by transnational corporations including Union Carbide and Pfizer. CCR "has considered possibilities for a large group settlement encompassing the claims of those individuals who have been exposed to asbestos and who may in the future contract an asbestos-related disease."[20]

Despite the difficulties for Agent Orange vets in the Reagan-Bush courts, they have found unexpected allies in the 21 state attorneys general who recently joined the *Ivy* case as 21 *amici curiae*, in the Appeals Court.[21] In their brief, the attorneys general argue that the *Ivy* case should not have been removed from Texas where it was filed by Texans against a Texas corporation. Furthermore, they assert, since there were no federal issues involved, removing it to a federal court was a violation of a state's right to maintain an independent judiciary.

The *Ivy* case brings vital issues into focus. On one side of this protracted struggle are the due process rights of victims, and the rights of states to exercise control over the corporations which impact the lives of their citizens. On the other side are giant corporations and the Reagan-Bush judiciary. If the vets win, they will not regain their health or the time spent fighting in the courts, but they will get some justice and legitimate monetary compensation. If the corporations are victorious in the courtroom, they will win a license to kill. Either way, the struggle is not over with *Ivy*. With so much at stake, the loser is sure to appeal to the Supreme Court.

1992-93

GULF WAR SYNDROME: GUINEA PIGS AND DISPOSABLE GIs

Tod Ensign

So far, about 300 U.S. GIs who served with Operation Desert Storm in the [Persian] Gulf have reported an array of chronic health ailments since they returned home. Some health experts fear that thousands more may develop similar problems in the years ahead.

The rapidity with which the Gulf vets have come forward to demand diagnosis and care contrasts with the earlier instances of service-related disease. The recent vets benefit from the legacy of Agent Orange-affected Vietnam veterans, some of whom have spent years challenging government stonewalling and fighting for health care to treat the effects of the toxic herbicide.[1]

Another factor at work may be the high number of reservists in

Operation Desert Storm — the first war in which the U.S. military employed its Total Force Concept. Under this plan, active-duty and reserve units were deployed together and cooperated closely. After Iraq invaded Kuwait, a quarter of a million members of the National Guard and Reserves were activated and 106,000 of them were sent to the Gulf, where reservists accounted for roughly a third of all ground combat troops. While active-duty GIs might be reluctant to complain for fear of retaliation in an era when force levels are being "down-sized," reservists are free from that concern. They are also more likely to have access to support networks, media, and non-military medical systems.

Previously, when GIs reported cancers and other health problems potentially linked to fallout from nuclear bomb tests or Agent Orange, they met indifference and outright hostility. This time, the government has at least *appeared* concerned about the Gulf vets' health allegations. Congress has already held two brief hearings and both military and the Department of Veterans Affairs hospitals have examined a number of these seriously ill vets.

In November 1992, President Bush signed a law authorizing Veterans Affairs to encourage Gulf vets to seek free medical evaluations and to establish a national health registry which can help Veterans Affairs track long-term health trends. One serious shortcoming, however, is that active-duty GIs will not be allowed to participate in this registry. Veterans Affairs director of epidemiology explained, excluding up to two-thirds of those at risk: "It would be too expensive," she told American Legion lobbyist Steve Robertson, "to include both groups."[2] After the Vietnam War, Veterans Affairs had resisted a similar program. Several years and much valuable data were lost before Congress finally ordered the department to create an Agent Orange Registry. Once it did, nearly 220,000 Vietnam veterans participated. Whether current government cooperation is simply a more sophisticated technique of crisis management, or reflects a genuine attempt to determine and treat service-related illness remains to be seen.

Possible Causes Identified

What has become known as the "Gulf War Syndrome" may actually result from a combination of factors, including:

- Smoke and pollution from some 600 oil-field petrochemical fires that burned in Kuwait for as long as eight months after the U.S.-led forces attacked Iraq.
- Two vaccines, pentavalent botulinum-toxoid and anthrax, and a medication, pyridostigmine bromide, which were designed as antidotes for biological or nerve gas weapons.
- Aerial spraying of pesticides over U.S. military bases in Saudi Arabia.
- Spraying of diesel oil to control dust around U.S. military bases in Saudi Arabia.
- Radiation exposure from depleted uranium used in some high velocity shells fired by M1A1 Abrams tanks and A-10 Thunderbolt fighter bombers.
- Portable heaters that used leaded gasoline and diesel fuel inside unventilated tents.
- Wholesale detonation of Iraqi ammunition depots without first determining whether or not they held toxic materials.
- Leishmaniasis – a parasitic infection spread by sand-flies.

Possible War Crime

The most controversial of the possible causes of the syndrome are the two drugs – pyridostigmine bromide and pentavalent botulinum-toxoid vaccine – neither of which had cleared the required Food and Drug Administration (FDA) review for new drugs.

Some Americans are vaguely aware that this country signed the Nuremberg Charter, which provided the legal basis for prosecuting Nazi leaders at the end of World War II. Fewer know of its companion treaty, the Nuremberg Code, aimed at preventing future human experimentation of the sort practiced by some German physicians. It is "absolutely essential," the code states, to obtain informed and voluntary consent for any medical treatment. There is no exception for wartime conditions or because soldiers are involved.

When the military decided to use the two unapproved drugs in the Gulf, it cited "military necessity," and petitioned the FDA to waive consent requirements. Although the FDA quickly acceded, some military advisers argued that the Pentagon had not needed the agency's permission to dispense the vaccines.

Just as U.S. bombs began falling on Baghdad, the Public Citizen Health Research Group (PCHRG) sued on behalf of unnamed soldier "John Doe" to enjoin the Pentagon from giving GIs the vaccines without first obtaining informed consent. U.S. District Court Judge Stanley Harris denied the public interest group an injunction to stop the program. "The decision to use unapproved drugs," he said, "is precisely the type of military decision that courts have refused to second guess."[3] The judge was following a number of precedents where courts have refused to make rulings that might interfere with military operations.[4]

When PCHRG appealed to the Circuit Court of Appeals,[5] the military shifted its position and claimed that the injection of the botulinum vaccine was only given with consent. Apparently, the government defense lawyers felt that since the anthrax vaccine enjoyed FDA approval, they didn't need to deal with the issue of consent to its use. "The Central Command," the Pentagon told the court, "decided to administer the pentavalent botulinum-toxoid on a voluntary basis."

We have learned that these representations were lies. Four Gulf War veterans testified before a September 1992 House Veterans Affairs Committee hearing that they had been forced to take the vaccine. Phillip Abbatessa, of East Boston, quoted his army superiors: "They said that if I didn't take the vaccination, then I was under UCMJ (Uniform Code of Military Justice) action" (i.e., subject to court martial). Sgt. Venus Hammack, of Lowell, Mass., told the committee that she was held down and forcibly given the vaccine against her will. A third vet, Frank Landy, of Nashua, N.H., also reported that he was ordered to take vaccinations on two occasions. Paul Perrone, of Methuen, Mass., told the committee that he wasn't told until two weeks after his vaccination that it was supposed to be voluntary.[6] Numerous other Gulf vets interviewed also reported that they were never asked for their consent and most did not know what vaccines they had been given.

One Army Reserve doctor refused to serve in the Gulf, citing international law and medical ethics. Dr. Yolanda Huet-Vaughn, 40, of Kansas City, Kan., whose defense was organized by Citizen Soldier, attempted to prove during her 1991 court-martial for desertion that, as a physician, she had a duty under the Nuremberg Code, not to vaccinate GIs without their informed consent. The military judge barred all evidence of international law from her trial.[7] The jury sentenced the mother of three small children to 30 months – the most severe prison term received by any Gulf War resister. A strong international campaign of support won her release after she had served eight months. The appeals court subsequently affirmed the lower court's refusal to enjoin the military.

Early Warnings

One of the first alarms that health problems might afflict Gulf veterans was sounded soon after the war by four military doctors. Writing in the *New England Journal of Medicine*, they warned that although most returning vets were unlikely to contract infectious diseases, it might be years before such diseases appeared.[8]

In January 1991, as the war was beginning, the Department of Defense circulated a detailed memo to all medical service staff, warning them to be alert for a range of GI health problems including reactions to anthrax and botulism injections, leishmaniasis, and effects from oil fires.[9]

As the war was ending, a panel of scientists at the Naval Medical Research Institute's Toxicology Detachment at Wright-Patterson Air Force Base in Ohio, compiled a comprehensive list of possible health problems from the oil-field fires. After consulting oil company experts who had extensive experience with oil-field fires and related environmental hazards, the panel identified several "agents of concern" including combustion products from burning oil wells and volatile hydrocarbon compounds in crude oil, both of which can be life threatening when inhaled. The military scientists urged that people working near such fires be given respirators, eye goggles, and special gas detectors. Citing the report, American Legion lobbyist Steve Robertson charged that although the Pentagon had known for 18 months about the potential health hazards, it did little to identify or protect vets at risk. It is unclear whether the navy report was widely circulated among various federal agencies.[10]

The Pentagon attracted some unwanted publicity to the health issue with its November 1991 announcement that none of the 540,000 Desert Storm GIs should donate blood until at least 1993. This action came after 28 vets were diagnosed with leishmaniasis, a potentially fatal disease transmitted by tiny sand-flies. Often called "tropica," leishmaniasis can affect the bone marrow, spleen, and liver, causing symptoms such as high fever, fatigue, weakness, and abdominal pain. The symptoms can range from mild to acute. The only reliable test for detection involves painful extraction of bone marrow, followed by an elaborate 47-hour lab analysis.

A Pentagon flyer circulated to Gulf veterans, "Briefing for Soldiers Returned from S.W.A. [Southwest Asia] – Leishmaniasis," falsely claimed that the disease is "not dangerous to your health and a normal healthy body will control the infection without medical treatment." The memo played down concern by urging that reservists "not make a special visit about this disease." If they choose to see a private doctor, the memo reminded, it would be at their own expense.

In October 1992, Chief of Infectious Diseases at Walter Reed Army Medical Center, Dr. Charles Oster, estimated that between one and three percent of the 400,000 Gulf ground troops (4,000-12,000 people) were exposed to the blood parasite.[11] Apparently, Oster's warnings were not appreciated in some circles; he has made no further public statements since this news report.

The American Legion, the nation's largest veterans' organization, published a list of suspected symptoms and a copy of a Veterans Affairs disability claim form in its May 1992 membership magazine. This action, which reached 3.2 million people, represents a significant shift for the politically conservative organization. During the early years of the Agent Orange controversy, the Legion, along with other veterans' groups, failed to challenge the deceptions practiced by the Pentagon and Veterans Affairs.

Since the article, said Legion director of National Veterans Affairs John Hanson, Gulf veterans have contacted many of the Legion's claim officers. "At this point, we don't really know what is causing all these problems," he noted, "but that doesn't mean that nothing's wrong."[12]

Hanson believes that while Veterans Affairs is genuinely interested in seeking answers, the military has been dragging its feet. "Exit physicals for Gulf War veterans were often little more than a paperwork formality," *The American Legion* magazine reported. "Some vets were even allowed to waive their exit physicals so that they could get home faster."[13]

Concern about the quality of exit physicals was buttressed by a General Accounting Office report published in October 1992, which found that many veterans – especially from the Navy and Air Force – were not given physicals when they left the military. "The absence of a separation exam," the report concluded, "can make it difficult for a veteran to prove a claim [later] if he or she didn't seek treatment for the condition... during military service."[14]

Clusters of Illness

The two largest clusters of ailing Gulf veterans to come forward so far are 79 Navy Seabees assigned to Camp 13 in Saudi Arabia and 80 members of the Indiana National Guard. The army sent a team of specialists in occupational medicine, epidemiology, psychiatry, and dentistry to examine each of the Indianans. In its July 1992 report, the team concluded "that the documentable medical problems... in this group are typical of the general population." In subsequent media interviews, these doctors insisted that the reservists suffered only from "mental stress."[15]

The other large cluster of the mysterious syndrome is 79 Georgia Seabees who served together in the Gulf. Four of the reservists told the *Atlanta Journal-Constitution* that they are unable to work at their former civilian jobs because of their illness.[16] Some navy doctors believe that about 25 of the ill Seabees suffer from leishmaniasis. "I'm trying to identify a set of symptoms and physical signs that defines the illness," said Lt. Commander Chris Ohl of Bethesda Naval Hospital.

That task is not made easier by the fact that many physicians and scientists disagree about what medical tests and procedures should be used in evaluating these veterans. Reserve Major Richard Haynes of New Albany, Ind., who has been actively trying to inform his fellow reservists about Gulf War health problems, believes that military researchers are not performing the relevant tests. "The Indiana reservists, for example, should have had tests for nerve conductivity, functional liver capacity, and for brain damage." Working on his own, Haynes has located over 160 Gulf veterans in 25 states who report some, or all, of the symptoms associated with the Gulf War syndrome.[17]

Just how many veterans are actually sick seems to depend, in part, on how aggressively government agencies look for them. A Veterans Affairs study of about 3,000 Gulf vets processed through Fort Devens, Mass., found that about 17 percent suffered from some or all of the ailments reported by vets elsewhere. "It's very preliminary," said Veterans Affairs psychologist Jessica Wolfe, "but we're seeing a number of people from units throughout New England that seem, at least on the surface, to have problems similar to [other] veterans."[18]

Depleted Uranium Shells Another Hazard

Among other possible contributing factors to the Gulf War Syndrome is radiation from depleted uranium high-velocity shells. Thousands of these dense projectiles were fired by M1A1 Abrams tanks and A-10 Thunderbolt fighter bombers to penetrate tank armor. On impact, radioactive oxidized uranium is released into the air. A May 24, 1991, army memorandum from the Armament, Munitions, and Chemical Command states: "Depleted Uranium presents a possible hazard [because] it is a heavy metal that can be toxic if ingested or inhaled. [It] becomes a hazard only when burned either by fire or with the heat of impact in a target area."

The army has admitted that at least 62 GIs were exposed to the radiation. Veterans Affairs specialist Dr. Belton Burrows examined 12 reservists from New Jersey's National Guard who were exposed to depleted uranium, but found no evidence that any of the men were harmed by the radiation. One of the exposed vets, Mark Panzera, attributes the headaches, fatigue, and chronic diarrhoea he now suffers to the uranium-laced dust in tanks he helped prepare for shipment back to the United States. The reservists' Congressmember, Representative Chris Smith (Rep.-N.J.) wants any veteran exposed to depleted uranium included in the Veterans Affairs' Gulf Registry. The army has no plans to track this group. "We feel as though we have run this about as far as it needs to run," said Col. Peter Myers, radiological consultant to the Army Surgeon General.[19]

Another subject of sharp debate is whether female vets or the wives of returning vets have suffered increased health problems, such as miscarriage, gynecological infections, or birth defects. Four women from Fort Hood, Texas, who served together in the Gulf reported persistent gynecological infections, abnormal pap smears, and cervical problems requiring biopsies. The women blame their new ailments on their Gulf service. The army's response? "There is no developing pattern of these problems at Fort Hood," said a spokesperson.[20]

East Boston vet Phillip Abbatessa told the House veterans panel in Boston, "I know that a lot of women at Fort Campbell, Kentucky [where he served] are having a hard time carrying children. There were a lot of miscarriages this year." Late in 1991, the antiwar Military Families Support Network announced that they were receiving many reports of miscarriage from female GIs and veterans' wives. In December, the Army Surgeon General's office denied that either group was suffering abnormal numbers of miscarriages. Major General Ronald Blanck claimed that the current miscarriage rate (about eight percent) was the same as it had been before the war and was about half the national average.[21]

Clearly, the military, with hard-liner Blanck as point man, is gearing up to defend itself. "The health of the military during Desert Storm," he testified on September 16, 1992, to the House panel, "was better than in any previous [war]." Discounting lack of FDA approval, Blanck vigorously defended the use of botulism vaccinations and pyridostigmine bromide. "They were not and are not experimental. They are well known and have been in use for many years," he argued. Interestingly, he didn't claim, as the Pentagon did before the Court of Appeals, that only GIs who consented were vaccinated.

The good doctor also dismissed other possible causes of the reported illnesses including oil fire pollution and other chemical hazards. In his view, the intense heat of the oil-field fires burned off most of the toxins. "The big smoke plumes that everyone saw were almost pure carbon; we didn't find volatile compounds that would [make us] really worry," he reported.

Finally, Blanck noted that nearly all of the 300 vets who have reported health problems so far were reservists, perhaps implying that somehow they are more prone to complain or be injured. He concludes, citing no evidence and backed by no studies, that, "Although there are a few exceptions, generally those on active duty do not have these symptoms."

As always, the Pentagon has an array of "experts" on hand to testify that no scientific evidence links the Gulf vets' health problems to their military service. When the House Veterans Affairs committee held its first hearing on the syndrome in September 1992, Dr. Lewis Kuller, an epidemiologist at the University of Pittsburgh, assured the panel that the only known health effect from Gulf duty is a small number of leishmaniasis cases. "I'm very concerned that there will be continuing efforts to generate 'new epidemics' that are supposedly related to the oil fires." Kuller also disparaged the creation of a Gulf Registry, claiming it would not provide any answers for worried veterans.[22]

The Environmental Protection Agency officer who led the federal interagency Air Pollution Assessment team to Kuwait acknowledged that emissions from the many oil-field fires could cause acute and chronic health effects. Jim Makris testified that, nonetheless, his team found "no levels of [toxic] chemicals at levels high enough to merit a public health concern."[23]

Other scientists, however, were less eager to dismiss health risks. Professor William Thilly, affiliated with MIT's Center for Environmental Health, questioned some of the government scientists' conclusions. "I find that the Petroleum Toxicity Task Force interpreted their [mandate] very narrowly. For instance, their focus on volatile polycyclates. The volatile chemicals do not concentrate the greatest concentrations for exposed persons. It's the non-volatiles which are bound to the particulates that [we] breathe deep into our lungs," stated Thilly. He recommended that the medical records of veterans with health complaints be grouped according to chemicals to which they may have been exposed. He also urged the government to consider that some veterans may be hypersensitive to vaccines and other chemicals.[24]

Indeed, several other independent scientists have suggested that some Gulf veterans may be suffering from "Multiple Chemical Sensitivity" (MCS). Dr. Theron Randolph, of Dallas, who is considered both a founder of modern epidemiology and the creator of the MCS diagnosis, examined two Gulf vets and determined petroleum poisoning. Dr. Alfred Johnson of the Environmental Health Center in Dallas, concluded that pollutants other than oil fires and spills may be a factor in the veterans' illnesses. Johnson's clinic is a national leader in treating MCS sufferers for a variety of illnesses after acute or long-term exposure to chemicals. Dr. Janet Levatin, a Boston environmental medicine specialist, confirmed that many of the vets' symptoms are consistent with patients exposed to petrochemicals, hydrocarbons, combustion gases, and pesticides.[25]

Forecasting the Future

Despite the flurry of publicity and the support of some Congress-members, ailing GIs and vets face a long, hard fight if they are to receive adequate medical care and disability compensation. The precedents set by the treatment of Agent Orange and nuclear test victims are not encouraging. It is still not in the military's economic or public relations interest to admit insufficient regard for the health and safety of those who served. Furthermore, the demands on the public purse have intensified over the last decade and both the Pentagon and the Department of Veterans Affairs (formerly the Veterans Administration) know that the salad days of the Carter-Reagan-Bush era are over. The vets will have to prove that their illnesses are service-related — a feat made more difficult by the lack of thorough medical exit examinations and insufficient monitoring and data collection.

In the Gulf vets' favor, however, veterans' organizations are more united and experienced in advocating veterans' claims than in the past.

One of the most important issues to be resolved in the months ahead will be the kinds of tests and procedures Veterans Affairs and military doctors use in evaluating claimants. The law establishing the Gulf War Veterans Health Registry required only that veterans shall receive a "health examination and consultation." Unless veterans and their advocates are vigilant, the government may get away with providing only superficial exams that will not detect any of the more subtle or complex health problems from which these veterans may be suffering.

The Agent Orange experience teaches that it is essential that independent medical personnel and scientists are involved from the beginning to watchdog every step the government takes. The stakes are high and the potential cost, both in lives and dollars, is enormous.

Operation Desert Storm has already taken a horrific toll on the people of Iraq and Kuwait. Will Gulf War veterans be added to this tally in the years ahead? Does the United States have the political will to look honestly at this issue?

We now know that the manufacturers of Agent Orange worked closely with the Pentagon and Veterans Affairs to conceal data about human health effects. One brave EPA scientist, Cate Jenkins, recently charged that a key Monsanto Company study of herbicide health effects was fraudulent.[26] The federal courts used this phony study to justify the grossly inadequate settlement of the Agent Orange class action in 1984. Given their histories and what is at stake, it would not be surprising to discover that Hoffman-LaRoche and other manufacturers of the vaccines given GIs are working behind the scenes to contain the government investigation of Gulf veterans' health problems.

Recently, the parents of an ailing GI from Florida wrote Representative Joe Kennedy (Dem.-Mass.) about their son, Ron. "Since returning home, [his] mental abilities have deteriorated to the point of [being] life-threatening. During this time, his physical appearance [also] became alarming. His hair began to fall out, weight loss, a bleeding ear, some hearing loss, aching joints, constant flu-like symptoms, and bouts of diarrhoea. We were struck to see a 22 year-old man look like a man in his mid-30s... Ron and many people like him put their young lives on the line... All they ask in return is that... our country stand by them, to find out what this Desert Storm illness is and to help the soldiers in need whatever the cost."

1992-93

BUSH ADMINISTRATION USES CIA TO STONEWALL IRAQGATE INVESTIGATION

Jack Colhoun

In House floor speeches, Rep. Henry González has documented how pre-Gulf War U.S. policy helped Iraq develop weapons of mass destruction. But President George Bush, taking a page from one of the darkest chapters of the Nixon presidency, has enlisted the CIA as part of his campaign to derail the Texas Democrat's Iraqgate investigation. The CIA is investigating González for revealing allegedly secret intelligence information, which it claims has harmed U.S. national security interests.

Involving the CIA in domestic political affairs is one of the few remaining taboos in U.S. politics, and so far, Bush has gotten away scot-free with it. His predecessor, Richard Nixon, was forced to resign a few days after the infamous "smoking gun" tape revealed that he had instructed White House Chief of Staff H. R. Haldeman to tell CIA Director Richard Helms to refuse to cooperate with the FBI's investigation of Watergate.[1]

While the media and the Washington pundits have duly reported the CIA's investigation of González, they have failed to note the resemblance between the way Bush and Nixon instigated domestic involvement of the CIA to protect their administrations. Nor have the media explored the ominous political implications of Bush — the first former CIA director elected president — using the agency to discredit his political foes.

The House Banking Committee, which González chairs, began looking into pre-Gulf War U.S. policy toward Iraq in 1990. "We have determined that your statements in the *Congressional Record* on July 7, 1992, included information from a top secret compartmented and particularly sensitive document dated September 4, 1989, to which we gave your staff access," CIA Director Robert Gates wrote in a July 24 letter to González. "Because of the sources and methods underlying that information, I will ask for a damage assessment to determine the impact of the disclosure." Adm. William O. Studeman, acting CIA director while Gates was abroad, informed González in a July 28 letter that the CIA's Office of Security would also assess González's House floor speeches of July 21 and July 27, 1992. Studeman claimed that González revealed other top secret intelligence information in these speeches.

The maverick Mexican American lawmaker from San Antonio, Texas, angrily denied the CIA's charges. "Your insinuation that I have revealed Top secret, compartmented information is inflammatory and without merit," González declared in a July 30 letter to Gates. "In fact, I have taken great pains to ensure that all information I have placed in the *Congressional Record* is of the broadest nature and readily available from public sources."

González added he was "extremely disappointed that the CIA was allowing itself to be used to build a smokescreen around the president's flawed policies. The CIA should be above involving itself in the political problems of the administration."

González also charged that since spring, the CIA has not

cooperated with the House Banking Committee. Attorney General William Barr, in a May 15, 1992, letter to the Texas Democrat, announced that the administration would no longer turn over classified documents to González's committee without "specific assurances" that he won't make the information public.

González, who has made public more classified U.S. documents than anyone since Daniel Ellsberg leaked the "Pentagon Papers," believes Bush is using the CIA to taint the Iraqgate investigation. Again the parallel is clear. In 1971, Nixon's White House "Plumbers," led by CIA operative E. Howard Hunt, launched a campaign to discredit former Pentagon analyst Ellsberg and even broke into his psychiatrist's office to search for incriminating dirt.

Meanwhile, Republicans on Capitol Hill escalated their vilification campaign against González. House Minority Leader Robert Michel (Rep.-Ill.) introduced a resolution in the House on August 4 that calls on the House Ethics Committee to investigate González's release of documents, citing the CIA probe of the 32-year House veteran. Michel charged that González had violated the House code of conduct, but he failed to note that lawmakers who disclose classified information on the House or Senate floor are exempted from the federal law against making intelligence secrets public.

Although the attacks against González continue, the growing body of evidence he is disclosing makes it increasingly difficult for the Bush administration to dismiss the allegations. And that, González believes, is why Bush unleashed the CIA.

The Substance of González's Charges

González rejects Bush's contention that U.S. policy was designed "to encourage Saddam Hussein to join the family of nations."

"The Bush administration," González charged in a July 27 speech, "sent U.S. technology to the Iraqi military and to many Iraqi military factories, despite overwhelming evidence showing that Iraq intended to use the technology in its clandestine nuclear, chemical, biological, and long-range missile programs." He quoted U.S. intelligence documents which show the administration knew that the Cleveland, Ohio, Matrix Churchill Corporation, and the Atlanta branch of the Italian Banca Nazionale del Lavoro (BNL) were the cornerstones of a secret Iraqi arms technology procurement network in the United States.

The administration's pro-Baghdad policy, spelled out in National Security Directive-26, adopted on October 2, 1989, was based on promoting U.S. trade with Iraq. The Commerce Department routinely approved applications from U.S. companies for the export to Iraq of "dual-use" technology, which has civilian and military applications.

"While the [Bush] policy did not permit the sale of bombs or something of that nature that would blow up," González declared in a July 21 speech, "it clearly allowed the sale of the equipment needed to make them. The administration knew what Saddam Hussein was doing... The head of Iraq's ambitious military industrialization efforts was Saddam's brother-in-law, Hussein Kamil, who directed the flow of over $2 billion in BNL commercial loans to various high-profile Iraqi weapons projects."

The progressive Texas Democrat contends that at a November 8, 1989, meeting, the Bush administration used a secret CIA report in an internal battle. The issue was whether to provide Iraq with $1 billion in loan guarantees to buy U.S. farm exports issued by the Department of Agriculture's Commodity Credit Corporation (CCC). Previously, the Export-Import Bank and other federal agencies opposed full funding for Iraq because its deteriorating economy made Baghdad a poor credit risk.

"This time the CCC program for Iraq was approved," González said in a July 7 speech. "The CIA report shows that unless the full $1 billion CCC program was approved, the president's goal of improving relations with Saddam Hussein as spelled out in NSD-26 would be frustrated." BNL-Atlanta made financial arrangements for the CCC program for Iraq.

The CIA report, González pointed out, "indicates that BNL loans were used to fund Iraq's clandestine military procurement network... in the United States and Europe. The report indicates that several of the BNL-financed front companies in the network were secretly procuring technology for Iraq's missile programs and nuclear, bio- logical and chemical weapons programs."

The House Judiciary Committee, after several hearings, called on [Attorney General] Barr July 9, 1992, to appoint an independent counsel to investigate Iraqgate. This move had been boosted when

Frank DeGeorge, inspector general for the Commerce Department, admitted at a June 23, 1992, House Judiciary Committee hearing that Commerce Department officials altered information on 66 export licenses for Iraq which were turned over to congressional investigators. The export licenses were changed from "VEHICLES DESIGNED FOR MILITARY USE" to "COMMERCIAL UTILITY CARGO TRUCKS."

But Barr took a hard line when, on August 1 — for the first time since the Ethics in Government Act created the independent counsel mechanism — he rejected a request for an appointment. Instead, the Justice Department, he asserted, would continue its investigation of Iraqgate. Barr called the charges outlined by the House Judiciary Committee too "vague" to justify an independent counsel.

"First the attorney general denounces and obstructs congressional investigations and now blocks inquiries by a special counsel," González responded the same day. "Barr is playing a dangerous game in a desperate effort to protect the Bush administration."

1992

NOTES

Chemical-Biological Warfare, Medical Experiments, and Population Control

1. "'Germ Warfare' in El Salvador?" *Daily World*, Feb. 17, 1982.
2. San Francisco Committee for Health Rights in Central America, *El Salvador 1985: Health, Human Rights and the War* (A Report of the Third U.S. Public Health Commission to El Salvador), p. 11.
3. "Dengue Epidemic: All Out Against... A Mosquito," *Barricada International*, Oct. 3, 1985, p.6; "Dengue: Another Facet of the War?" *Barricada International*, Nov. 21, 1985, p. 13.
4. Lincoln Detox (a drug detoxification program at Lincoln Hospital, New York City), "Dope is Death," paper prepared for National Hearings on the Heroin Epidemic, Washington, D.C., June 29, 1976.
5. Much of this discussion is condensed from Louis Wolf's article, "This Side of Nuclear War: The Pentagon's Other Option," in *CAIB*, No. 17 (Summer 1982), pp.16-17. See also, Leonard A. Cole, "The Army's Secret Germ-War Testing," *The Nation*, Oct. 23, 1982.
6. Ellen Bulf, "Have Mosquitoes Been Drafted in a Secret War?" *In These Times*, Sept. 23-29, 1981, p. 22; and "U.S. Germ Warfare Tests Revealed — Target: Savannah, Georgia," *Revolutionary Worker*, Nov. 21, 1980.
7. Marshall S. Shapo, *A Nation of Guinea Pigs: The Unknown Risks of Chemical Technology* (New York: Free Press 1979), p. 91; Ana María García, Study Guide for "La Operación" (a film about sterilization of Puerto Rican women), 1986, available from Cinema Guild, New York City.
8. Jessica Mitford, *Kind and Unusual Punishment: The Prison Business* (New York: Knopf, 1976), pp. 138-67.
9. Louis Lasagna, "Special Subjects in Human Experimentation," in Paul A. Freund, ed., *Experimentations with Human Subjects* (New York: George Brazilier, 1969), p. 262.

10. William Robbins, "Dioxin Tests Conducted on 70 Philadelphia Inmates, Now Unknown, in 60s," *New York Times*, July 17, 1983.

11. Mitford, *op. cit.*, n. 8, pp. 157-67; John Lastala, "Atascadero: Dachau for Queers," *Advocate*, Apr. 25, 1972, pp. 11-13.

12. James H. Jones, *Bad Blood: The Tuskegee Syphilis Experiment* (New York: The Free Press: 1980), p. 2.

13. *Ibid.*, p. 13.

14. See, generally, Pedro I. Aponte Vázquez, "*Yo Accuso! Tortura y Asesinato de Don Pedro Albizu Campos,*" (Bayamon, Puerto Rico: Movimiento Ecuménico Nacional de Puerto Rico, 1985); and Pedro I. Aponte Vázquez, "*Asesino Rhoads a Albizu?*" pamphlet, no date or publisher.

15. The Stockholm International Peace Research Institute, in a definitive study on chemical-biological warfare, found "little difference between offensive and defensive chemical-biological warfare research." Quoted in Charles Piller, "DNA — Key to Biological Warfare?" *The Nation*, Dec. 10. 1983, p. 598.

16. "Some common forms of vaccine production are very close technically to production of chemical-biological warfare agents and so offer easy opportunities for conversion." *Ibid.* See also, Alexander Hiam, "The Next Generation of Biological Weapons," *Science for the People*, May-June 1982, pp. 32-35; Robert Ruttman, "Strictly Anti-Human Chemical-Biological Warfare," *Science for the People*, May-June 1984, pp. 6-30.

17. Mark Crawford, "DoD to Reassess Bioweapons' Risks," *Science*, Feb. 27, 1987, p. 968.

18. DoD spokesperson, testifying before a House subcommittee, 1969, quoted in Robert Harris and Jeremy Paxman, *A Higher Form of Killing: The Secret Story of Chemical & Biological Warfare* (New York: Hill & Wang, 1982), p. 266.

19. *Ibid.*, pp. 241-66.

20. *Report of the President's Chemical Warfare Review Commission* (Washington: GPO, 1985), p. 69.

21. See Carl A. Larson, "Ethnic Weapons," *Military Review*, Nov. 1970; and see "DoD's Nerve Gas Sales Pitch," *CAIB*, No. 17, p. 25. It has been reported to the United Nations Commission for Namibia that South Africa is suspected of conducting research on diseases which only affect black people. Report for 1983-1984. See also A. Conadera, "Biological Weapons and Third World Targets," *Science for the People*, July-Aug. 1981, pp. 16-20.

22. Paul Wagman, "U.S. Goal: Sterilize Millions of World's Women," *St. Louis Post-Dispatch*, quoted in G. Esterman, "The Master Plan," *Womanews* (New York), Dec.-Jan. 1986-87, p. 15.

23. Ana María García, *op. cit.*, n. 7; Bonnie Mass, "Puerto Rico: A Case Study of Population Control," *Latin American Perspectives*, Fall 1977.

Cancer Warfare

1. Charles Piller and Keith R. Yamamoto, *Gene Wars: Military Control Over* the *New Genetic Technologies* (New York: Beech Tree Books/Morrow and Co., 1988), p. 50.
2. Louis Wolf, "This Side of Nuclear War," *CAIB*, (Summer 1982), p. 14.
3. The bureaucratic organization of NCI units changes. Some NCI contracts began before the VCP actually started. For simplicity, these contracts are referred to as VCP contracts when they continue under the VCP effort.
4. The author believes that the vast majority of scientists involved were and are well-intentioned colleagues whose ethics are not in question.
5. *U.S. Army Activity in the U.S. Biological Warfare Programs*, Vol. 11, Unclassified, Feb. 24, 1977, pp. I-C-4-5.
6. The U.S. treaty obligation was under the Geneva Convention on the Prohibition of the Development, Production, and Stockpiling of Bacteriological (Biological) and Toxin Weapons and on Their Destruction, signed at Washington and Moscow on April 10, 1972, and published in *Gene Wars, op. cit.*, n.1, pp. 162-63. This treaty specifically bound its parties [Article I] never to "develop, produce, or stockpile... microbial or other biological agents, or toxins whatever their origin or method of production of types and in quantities that have no justification for prophylactic, protective or other peaceful purposes." Thus, dangerous cancer viruses would be difficult to produce in "quantities that have no justification" unless a medical cover could be found. (Piller and Yamamoto, *op. cit.* n. 1).
7. *Special Virus Cancer Project Progress Report, 1972*, Etiology Area National Cancer Institute, U.S. Department of Health, Education, and Welfare (DHEW), Public Health Service, p. 33.
8. Erhard Geissler, ed., *Biological and Toxin Weapons Today* (New York: Oxford University Press, 1986), p. 22.
9. *The Viral Cancer Program Progress Report*, U.S. National Institutes of Health, June 1977, p. 272.
10. John Cookson and Judith Nottingham, *A Survey of Chemical and Biological Warfare* (New York: Modern Reader, 1969), p. 82.
11. Seymour Hersh, *Chemical and Biological Warfare* (New York: Bobbs-Merrill, 1968), p. 226.
12. *The Viral Cancer Program Progress Report*, U.S. National Institutes of Health, June 1977, pp. 272, 302.

13. *American Men and Women of Science* (New York: R.R. Bowker, 1976), p. 1097.
14. *Op. cit.*, n. 5, p. D2.
15. *Op. cit.*, n. 11, p. 128.
16. *Op. cit.*, n. 13, p. 358.
17. *Op. cit.*, n. 9, p. 52.
18. *Ibid.*, p. 302.
19. *Op. cit.*, n. 7, p. 7.
20. *Op. cit.*, n. 10, p. 82.
21. *Ibid.*, p. 91.
22. *Op. cit.*, n. 5.
23. *Science*, Vol. 204, June 22, 1979, p. 1287.
24. *Op. cit.*, n. 7, p. 114.
25. *Op. cit.*, n. 11, p. 255.
26. *Op. cit.*, n. 7, p. 32-3.
27. *Op. cit.*, n. 1, p. 117.
28. *Op. cit.*, n. 11, pp. 59-60.
29. *Op. cit.*, n. 5, p. I-C-4.
30. *Op. cit.*, n. 7, p. 68.
31. A retrovirus is a virus whose genetic material is composed of RNA instead of DNA and which must convert to a DNA form before it can reproduce. The human immunodeficiency viruses are retroviruses.
32. *Science*, Volume 193, July 23, 1976, p. 273.
33. *Ibid.*
34. H. Balner and W.I.B. Beveridge, eds., *Infections and Immunosuppression in Subhuman Primates* (Baltimore: Williams and Wilkins Company, 1970), p. 116.
35. "Proceedings of a Cancer Research Safety Symposium," DHEW Publication No. (NIH) pp. 76-890, Mar. 19, 1975.
36. *Ibid.*, p. 62.
37. *Op. cit.*, n. 1, p. 53.
38. *Op. cit.*, n. 11, p. 278-39.
39. *Ibid.*
40. J.B. Nielands, "Navy Alters Course at Berkeley," *Science for the People*, Nov.-Dec. 1988, p. 11.
41. "CIA May Have Tested Biological Weapons in New York in '50s, Church Says," *Washington Post*, Dec. 4, 1979, p. A7.
42. John Marks, *The Search for the "Manchurian Candidate"* (New York: McGraw Hill, 1980), pp. 74-75.
43. Church Committee Report, "Unauthorized Storage of Toxic Agents," Vol. 1, pp. 189-99.

Zimbabwe's Anthrax Epizootic

1. In June 1979, Rhodesia became Zimbabwe-Rhodesia; in April 1980, Robert Mugabe became head of majority-ruled Zimbabwe.
2. J. K. Cilliers, *Counter-Insurgency in Rhodesia* (London: Croom Helm, 1985), pp. 16-17.
3. Anthrax is a potentially fatal disease of humans and animals caused by the bacterium *Bacillus anthracis.* Unlike most bacteria, anthrax organisms form spores when exposed to air, which may remain infectious for decades. Humans contract anthrax by eating or inhaling the spores or by exposure to spores through cuts in the skin. The fatality rate of inhalation anthrax is 95 percent, of gastrointestinal anthrax 50 percent, and of cutaneous anthrax, five percent. The vast majority of anthrax cases in the world are cutaneous and are caused by handling contaminated meat.
4. Max Sterne, "Distribution and Economic Importance of Anthrax," *Federation Proceedings,* vol. 26, 1967, pp. 1493-95. Sterne, originally from South Africa, is one of the world's experts on anthrax and developed an animal anthrax vaccine in the 1930s which is used today.
5. See J. A. Lawrence, *et al.,* "The Effects of War on the Control of Diseases of Livestock in Rhodesia (Zimbabwe)," *Veterinary Record 1980,* vol. 107, pp. 82-85. Fifty percent of Rhodesia's land area, the agriculturally better land, was reserved for whites; 50 percent was reserved for Rhodesia's blacks, who made up over 90 percent of the population. The black areas were named Tribal Trust Lands at the time of the war, and are currently termed communal farming areas.
6. See Meryl Nass, "Anthrax Epizootic in Zimbabwe, 1978-1980: Due to Deliberate Spread?" *PSR Quarterly,* vol. 2, no. 4, December 1992.
7. Human cases for 1950-1963 were extracted from the *Annual Reports on the Public Health, for 1965-1977* from the Ministry of Health for Southern Rhodesia, Bulletin of diseases notified during months ended, and for 1978-1980 from the *Reports of the Secretary of Health,* Harare, Zimbabwe, Govt. Printer.
8. J.C.A. Davies, "A Major Epidemic of Anthrax in Zimbabwe" Part 1, *Central African Journal of Medicine,* vol. 29, 1983, pp. 8-12.
9. Allan Pugh and J.C.A. Davies, "Human Anthrax in Zimbabwe," *Salisbury Medical Bulletin* (supplement), vol. 68, 1990, pp. 32-33.
10. W.E. Kobuch, *et al,* "A Clinical and Epidemiological Study of 621 patients with anthrax in western Zimbabwe," *Salisbury Medical Bulletin, op. cit.,* pp. 34-38.
11. See the Food and Agriculture Organization (United Nations), *Animal Health Yearbooks,* V. Kouba, ed., Rome, Italy, 1979, 1980, 1981.

12. Lawrence, *op. cit.*, n. 5, p. 84.
13. Barton J. Bernstein, "The Birth of the U.S. Biological Warfare Program" *Scientific American,* vol. 256, pp. 116-21; and Bernstein, "Churchill's Secret Biological Weapon," *Bulletin of Atomic Scientists,* January/ February 1987, pp. 46-50; and Peter Williams and David Wallace, *Unit 731: Japan's Secret Biological Warfare in World War II* (New York: The Free Press, 1989), pp. 121-40.
14. Sterling Seagrave, *Yellow Rain* (New York: M. Evans and Co., 1981), pp. 167-68; and "Unauthorized Storage of Toxic Agents," hearings before the Select Committee to Study Governmental Operations With Respect to Intelligence Activities (the Church Committee), 94th Congress, September 16, 17, 18, 1975.
15. Meryl Nass, "The Labyrinth of Biological Defense," *PSR Quarterly, vol.* 1, no. 1, March 1991, pp. 24-30; and Stockholm International Peace Research Institute, *The Problem of Chemical and Biological Warfare, v. 2, CB Weapons Today* (New York: Humanities Press, 1973), pp. 79-90.
16. Cilliers, *op. cit.*, n. 2, p. 15.
17. A.O. Pugh and J.C.A. Davies, *op. cit.*, n. 9, p. 32.
18. Richard Falk, "Inhibiting Reliance on Biological Weaponry," in Susan Wright, ed., *Preventing a Biological Arms Race* (Cambridge, Mass.: MIT Press, 1990) pp. 248-51.
19. Bernstein, "Birth of...," and Bernstein, "Churchill's Secret...," *op. cit.*, n. 13, pp. 46-50.
20. Wright, *op. cit.*, n. 18, pp. 37-43.
21. Nass, *op. cit.*, n. 15; and Vera Rick, "Anthrax in the Urals," *Lancet,* vol., 339, 1992, pp. 419-20.
22. Meryl Nass, "Can Biological, Toxin and Chemical Warfare Be Eliminated?," *Politics and the Life Sciences, 1992,* vol. 11, no. 1, pp. 30-32.

U.S. Biological Warfare: The 1981 Cuba Dengue Epidemic

1. While it is beyond the scope of this article, it appears that the Afghan government and the Soviet government have accused the United States of very similar biological warfare in Afghanistan. Reports in February 1982 suggested that CIA operatives at a research center in Lahore, Pakistan, though pretending to be engaged in malaria eradication, were actually experimenting in the spread of dengue and yellow fever. The reports first appeared in *Literaturnaya Gazeta* on February 3, 1982, and were carried the next day by UPI.
2. See Warren Hinckle and William Turner, *The Fish Is Red*, p. 293.
   [*Editors' note: In his 1984 book,* Afghanistan — Washington's Secret War, *journalist Phillip Bonosky noted that in 1981, "Pakistan expelled a Dr. David*

R. Nalin, an American who headed what was called the 'malarial research center' near Lahore, charging that he was using those facilities to breed mosquitoes, not however to discover how to control malaria as announced, but how to cultivate even deadlier forms of it. Once the formula was found, the educated mosquitoes would be dropped over (or smuggled into) Cuba and Afghanistan." Bonosky adds, "They probably arrived in Cuba as dengue fever in 1981."]

Agent Orange: The Dirty Legal War at Home

1. Peter H. Schuck, *Agent Orange on Trial: Mass Toxic Disasters in the Courts* (Cambridge, Mass.: Harvard University Press, 1987). This is the most comprehensive account of the first Agent Orange case and its forced settlement by a judge.
2. Committee on Government Operations, "The Agent Orange Coverup: A Case of Flawed Science and Political Manipulation," House Report (H. Rep.), pp. 101-672.
3. *Ibid.*, p. 2.
4. *Ibid.*, p. 3.
5. Schuck, *op. cit.*, n. 1, p. 178.
6. *New York Times*, May 8, 1984, p. 134.
7. See affidavits submitted to the court in the *Ivy* case, CV-89-03361 (E.D.N.Y.), Plaintiffs' *Exhibit H*, EPA official Cate Jenkins, "Recent Scientific Evidence Developed After 1984 Supporting a Causal Relationship Between Dioxin and Human Health Effects"; and *Exhibit I*, Adm. Elmo Zumwalt, Commander of U.S. Naval Forces in Vietnam (1968-70). (Available from Greenpeace USA, 1436 U St., NW, Washington, DC 20009.)
8. See *Ryan v. Dow*, 618 F. Supp. for text of order, pp. 623-25. (E.D.N.Y. 1985).
9. See *Ryan v. Dow*, 781 F. Supp. 910 (E.D.N.Y. 1991).
10. Steven Labaton, "Five Years After Settlement, Agent Orange War Lives on," *New York Times*, May 18, 1989.
11. AOCAP memo, Oct. 4, 1991, from Dennis Rhoades, head of AOCAP to grantees, subject: "Court Issues Ruling in Ivy Case."
12. Brief for *Shirley Ivy, et al.*, No. 92-7575 (2d Cir.).
13. *Ibid.*
14. H. Rep. 101-672, p. 18.
15. See July 26, 1990, hearing of the Human Resources and Inter-governmental Relations Subcommittee, pp. 22-40.
16. Jeff Bailey, "Duelling Studies: How Two Industries Created a Fresh Spin On the Dioxin Debate," *Wall Street Journal*, Feb. 20, 1992, p. C12;

and David Lapp, "Defenders of Dioxin," *Multinational Monitor*, Oct. 1991, pp. 8-12.
17. Affidavit in *Ivy* case, CV-89-03361 (E.D.N.Y) p. 8.
18. House of Representatives, HRIRS, Committee on Government Operations, June 10, 1992, 102nd Congress.
19. Brief for the Center for Claims Resolution as *Amicus Curiae*, Oct. 30,1992, in *Ivy v. Diamond Shamrock.*, No. 92-7575 (2d Cir.), pp. 2-3.
20. *Ibid.*, pp. 2-3.
21. Brief *amici curiae* of the State of Alabama *(et al.)* in support of appellants, Sept. 16, 1992, No. 92-75 75 (2d Cir.).

Gulf War Syndrome: Guinea Pigs and Disposable GIs

1. Michael Uhl and Tod Ensign, *GI Guinea Pigs: How the Pentagon Exposed Our Troops to Dangers More Deadly Than War – Agent Orange & Atomic Radiation* (New York: Playboy Press, 1980), chapters 7-10.
2. Interview with author, Nov. 13, 1992.
3. *Doe v. Sullivan*, 754 F. Supp. 12 (D.C.D.C. 1991).
4. George J. Annas, "Changing the Consent Rules for Desert Storm," *New England Journal of Medicine*, Mar. 12, 1992, pp. 770-73.
5. *Doe v. Sullivan*, 938 F. 2d 1370 (D.C.Cir. 1991).
6. Dolores Kong, "Gulf Veterans Describe Lingering Health Woes," *Boston Globe*, Sept. 22, 1992, p. 1.
7. Citizen Soldier's cooperating attorneys Louis Font and Luther C. West are appealing the conviction, based in part on the judge's restrictive rulings. A decision is expected in 1993.
8. Drs. Lt. Col. Robert Gasser, Maj. Alan Magill, Col. Charles Oster, and Col. Edmund Tramont, "The Threat of Infectious Disease in Americans Returning from Operation Desert Storm," *New England Journal of Medicine*, Mar. 21, 1991, pp. 859-63.
9. Interview with American Legion's Steve Robertson, Nov. 13, 1992.
10. Nick Tate, "Military Knew of Chemical Dangers in the Gulf," *Boston Herald*, Aug. 6, 1992, p. 1.
11. "Test for Parasite Misses Many Gulf Vets," *Chicago Tribune*, Oct. 8, 1992.
12. Interview with author, October 1992.
13. "Gulf War Veteran: Document Ailments Now," *The American Legion*, May 1992, pp. 18-26.
14. "Missed Physicals Hurt Gulf War Veterans," *Times*, Nov. 2, 1992.
15. ABC-TV, "20-20", Aug. 29,1992.
16. "Gulf Vets Who Served in Same Camp Show Cluster of Mysterious Ailments," *Atlanta Journal-Constitution*, Oct. 19,1992.
17. Interview with author, Oct. 31, 1992.

18. Nick Tate, "Toxins Eyed In Mysterious Gulf War Ailments," *Boston Herald,* Aug. 3, 1992.
19. Soraya Nelson, "Radiation, Storm Illnesses Link Alleged," *Army Times,* Oct. 12, 1992, p. 28.
20. Sandra Evans, "Vet Groups Call for Study of Possible Desert Storm Illness," *Washington Post,* Apr. 29, 1992, p. All.
21. Katherine McIntire, "Surgeon General Says Miscarriage Rate Normal," *Army Times,* Dec. 9, 1991.
22. Testimony, House Veterans Affairs Committee, Subcommittee on Hospitals and Health Care, Sept. 16, 1992, Washington, D.C.
23. *Ibid.*
24. Testimony, House Veterans Affairs Committee, Subcommittee on Hospitals and Health Care, Sept. 21, 1992, Boston, Mass.
25. *Boston Herald, op. cit.,* n. 19.
26. Jeff Nesmith, "Monsanto Altered Dioxin Study, EPA Memo Says," *Indianapolis Star,* Mar. 23, 1990, p. A3.

Bush Administration Uses CIA To Stonewall Iraqgate Investigation

1. Barry Sussman, *The Great Cover-Up: Nixon and the Scandal of Watergate* (Arlington, Va.: Seven Locks Press, 1992), pp. 295-96; and Jack Colhoun, "Did Watergate Plumbers Deep-Six JFK?" (New York) *Guardian* newsweekly, June 24, 1992.

CONTRIBUTORS

JACK COLHOUN was the Washington correspondent for the (New York) *Guardian* newsweekly. He has a Ph.D. in U.S. history, specializing in post-World War II foreign and military policy.

TOD ENSIGN is the director of Citizen Soldier, a GI and veterans' rights advocacy organization based in New York City.

RICHARD HATCH is a research chemist who designs scientific instruments for use in biotechnology and related fields.

KEN LAWRENCE is a freelance writer who has written extensively on issues relating to the U.S. intelligence complex and government misconduct.

ROBERT LEDERER is a long-time anti-racism activist and investigative journalist, currently co-host of Health Action, on WBAI/Pacifica Radio.

A. NAMIKA is a freelance journalist who has written on Agent Orange and on the Bhopal, India, disaster.

MERYL NASS, M.D., is an expert on anthrax and biological warfare, who has testified several times on the subject before the U.S. Congress.

ELLEN RAY is a journalist and filmmaker, president of the Institute for Media Analysis, Inc., and a co-founder of *CovertAction*.

WILLIAM H. SCHAAP is an attorney and journalist, and a co-founder of *CovertAction*.

AMERIKA PSYCHO
Behind Uncle Sam's Mask of Sanity
By Richard Neville
Notorious for the *Oz* magazine 1960s censorship trials, Neville now takes aim at today's all-powerful U.S. culture, which through its movies, media, politics and foreign policy reveals a "disturbing identification with Imperial Rome, asserting the sanctity of its lifestyle, even as the icecaps melt." As we gear up for war, Neville warns, the "wounded Goliath is on the rampage," stuck in a "perilous psychic gridlock of us/them, good/evil."
ISBN 1-876175-62-1

LATIN AMERICA
From Colonization to Globalization
By Noam Chomsky
As Latin America hovers of the brink of a major social and economic crisis, Mexican-based professor of sociology, Heinz Dieterich, discusses some of the main political events in recent years with the internationally acclaimed philosopher, scholar and political activist, Noam Chomsky. "Gaining an understanding of what these last 500 years have meant is not simply a matter of becoming aware of history, it is a question of becoming aware of current processes." —Noam Chomsky
ISBN 1-876175-13-3

FORTHCOMING IN FALL 2003:

COVERT ACTION AND THE ROOTS OF TERRORISM
Edited by Ellen Ray and William H. Schaap
Bringing together a selection of key articles from *CovertAction*, the most authoritative international magazine in its field, this book examines the major political events and issues of the 1980s and 1990s, including covert U.S. interventions in Afghanistan, Central America, the Middle East, Grenada, Panama, Iraq and elsewhere.
Published in association with the Institute for Media Analysis, Inc.
ISBN 1-876175-26-5

oceanpress
e-mail info@oceanbooks.com.au
www.oceanbooks.com.au